Polymer
CLAY
for Everyone

GLOUCESTER MASSACHUSETTS

ROCKPORT PUBLISHERS

SUZANN THOMPSON

To my family with love and appreciation

First Published in the United States of America in 2001 by
Rockport Publishers, Inc.
33 Commercial Street
Gloucester, Massachusetts 01930
Telephone: 978-282-9590
Facsimile: 978-283-2742
www.rockpub.com

Publishing Director LAURA BAMFORD

Executive Editor MIKE EVANS
Senior Editor NINA SHARMAN
Managing Editor JANE DONOVAN

Art Director KEITH MARTIN
Executive Art Editor MARK WINWOOD
Designer LISA TAI
Cover Designer LEEANN LEFTWICH
Production PHILLIP CHAMBERLAIN

Photography DAVID SHERWIN

ISBN 1-56496-637-2
Produced by Toppan Printing Company Ltd
Printed and bound in China

contents

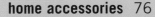

introduction

Polymer clay is truly a medium for everyone: it delivers the thrill of creativity to complete beginners, small children, hobbyists and professionals alike. With simple and inexpensive tools you can make beautiful buttons and beads, ornaments, gifts, miniatures, and more out of polymer clay. The projects you design can be as realistic or as fantastic as you can imagine.

Polymer clay can be used to make realistic imitations of real-life objects and creatures, and sometimes you can even be fooled into thinking that it's something that it's not. In the hands of experts, polymer clay can be transformed into delicious-looking breads and delicate blancmanges, life-like dolls that look as though they could sit up and greet you, Japanese netsukes (carved ornaments), apparent Bakelite®, fine ivory, jade and turquoise. Polymer clay designers have borrowed from and been inspired by lampwork and other glass-making techniques, metalworking, sugarcraft and even quilt piecing. These processes have been copied in polymer clay in a colour palette that cannot be matched by any of them.

We have doll-makers to thank for the initial development of polymer clay, but I have purposefully left doll- and figurine-making out of this book. Those arts are explored and explained in books and workshops by people who have much more expertise than I do.

As I designed the projects in this book, I re-read and studied *The New Clay* by Nan Roche (this was the book that launched a new era in polymer clay artistry and crafting); *The Art of Polymer Clay* by Donna Kato and *Making Doll's House Miniatures with Polymer Clay* by Sue Heaser. These are the original polymer clay sourcebooks. I also spent hours measuring the neighbour's cat and the living room fireplace, poring over books about decorative ornament and Christie's auction yearbooks, studying gemstones, buttons, art deco chinaware and nautical flags, and trying to remember everything I've ever learned from experience and from others about polymer clay. I hope that you enjoy making these projects as much as I enjoyed designing them.

Suzann Thompson

The vibrant designs, with their unique patterning and colour, featured on these pages show just a few of the exciting ideas that you can try using polymer clay.

1

materials & techniques

materials & techniques

Polymer clay is a plastic modelling material. Despite the word "clay" in its name, polymer clay doesn't contain any earthen clay. It hardens (or cures) permanently when baked in a home oven and you can achieve wonderful results using inexpensive tools, many of which can be found around the home as with so many other crafts. You can buy speed, as well as greater precision and ease, by investing in more expensive tools. It's up to you to decide exactly where you fall in this continuum of time versus money.

This section of the book includes a discussion of the different polymer clay brands, tools, supplies and techniques, many of which were used to make the projects in this book.

Samples of different polymer clays

Materials

Several different brands of polymer clay are available today. Choose the one that works best for your particular project.

FIMO®, FIMO®soft and MixQuick
(manufactured by Eberhard Faber)
FIMO is the most widely recognized polymer clay brand. It is now available in over 40 colours which include pearlized, transparent, stone-effect, translucent, fluorescent, glow-in-the-dark, as well as some metallic colours. Because of its slight stiffness, FIMO has always been a favourite of miniaturists and millefiori-makers, although its stone-effect colours are not ideal for millefiori. The formulation of FIMO has changed during the past few years to make it more pliable and easier to condition (see pages 15–16). It bakes to an almost semi-gloss finish.
FIMOsoft is much easier to condition than standard FIMO, but the colour range is not quite as good. MixQuick is a softening compound. When mixed at no more than a 1:4 ratio with standard polymer clay, it does not noticeably alter the colour.

Sculpey III®, Sculpey® and SuperSculpey®
(manufactured by Polyform Products)
Sculpey III is available in 40 colours including translucent, neon, pearlized and metallic. Although smooth and pliable, nevertheless you must knead it before you begin your project. The texture of Sculpey III makes it good for modelling and sculpting and it is easy to extrude using a clay gun. It bakes to a matte finish that sands beautifully.
Sculpey is only available in white. It is an economical modelling compound which can be painted after curing (hardening).

SuperSculpey is a beige sculpting compound that bakes to a ceramic-like finish. While it is favoured for its good tooling and sculpting qualities, it can also be used as a softening compound for stiff or crumbly polymer clays.

Sculpey Super-Flex (Polyform Products) A very flexible clay, Sculpey Super-Flex differs from other polymer clays in that it must be warmed before conditioning (see pages 15–16).

Premo!™ Sculpey (Polyform Products) Premo! (formerly known as Clay Factory Clay) is a newcomer to the polymer clay market. It was developed, with much input from polymer clay users, by the artist Marie Segal. Because colour-mixing is such a large part of polymer clay artistry, Premo!'s colours include several from the artist's palette – burnt umber, raw sienna, zinc yellow and cadmium red, to name but a few. In addition to these, Premo! also offers a range of translucent, pearlized, fluorescent, glow-in-the-dark and metallic polymer clay colours. It is pliable and very easy to work with, but still requires conditioning (see pages 15–16).

SAFETY NOTE

Polymer clay is made of PVC (polyvinylchloride) particles suspended in a plasticizer. It is a chemical compound and should be treated with care. Please read and follow the manufacturers' recommendations on the product labels.

Granitex Stone Colors (Polyform Products)
No matter how much you knead it, Granitex has a mottled stone look. The effect is achieved with fibrous chunks that are mixed with a translucent base. It is fine for modelling and gives a subtle pastel granite effect. It is not so well suited for millefiori or other techniques where you slice the clay because the blade catches the fibrous chunks and then pulls them down, which makes a concentrated colour line at the end of the cut.

Cernit (T & F Kunststoffe GmbH)
Cernit is a translucent polymer clay that is available in a range of over 50 colours including pearlized, metallic, neon and nature-effect. An opaque white is also offered, since regular white is the equivalent to translucent in the other brands. The pearlized or glamour colours are very pearly. As a rule, Cernit is very soft and some of the colours are very, very soft. After baking, it is strong and has a semi-gloss finish.

Because of its translucency, Cernit has been favoured for doll-making and a doll colour collection of polymer clay is offered within the range.

Other brands
You can find several other brands of polymer clay with varying success in different countries. The brands to look for are Modello, Formello, Modelene and Creall-therm.

Tools and equipment

Polymer clay actually presents so many possibilities that to give a list of tools and equipment seems to be quite daunting. Luckily, you don't need to have all these tools to achieve good results. In the list that follows, I have marked what I consider to be the essential tools and equipment with a symbol ★. On page 15 you will find a list of standard equipment and supplies for making the projects in this book and these are shown in the photograph on this page with a key to their identification.

Your hands ★
Use your hands to condition clay, and to roll and model it. Don't be afraid of using clay: you can't hurt it, so twist it, turn it, squash it and roll it. Warm, strong hands condition clay so much faster. If you have cold hands, follow the suggestions for warming clay on page 15.

Standard equipment and supplies ★

1 *Clean, white copier paper*	***8*** *Craft knife with curved blade*
2 *Scissors*	***9*** *Long, thin blade*
3 *Home-made and commercial ball styluses*	***10*** *Print roller or brayer*
4 *Ceramic tile*	***11*** *Ruler*
5 *Pencil*	***12*** *Two-part epoxy*
6 *Wool and darning needles and other piercing tools*	***13*** *Extra-strong adhesive*
7 *Wet/dry sandpaper*	***14*** *Baking tray*

Work surface ★

Your work surface should be clean and smooth, and hard enough to withstand cutting blades. Ceramic or stone tiles or slabs, glass, lucite or kitchen worktop laminate are all good surfaces. Cool materials, such as ceramic or stone, can stiffen too-soft clay and, by the same token, warm surfaces can keep stiff clay more pliable.

Ceramic tiles Whenever accuracy is important or whenever you have fragile parts to make, you will find that ceramic tiles are an especially good surface because you can build and bake your project on the tile. For thin, flat pieces, place a sheet of white paper and a ceramic tile on top of the piece during and after baking to prevent warping.

Clean white copier paper placed on one of the surfaces mentioned above is an ideal base for making small projects. You can lift and move the paper without disturbing the project, and you may also bake your projects on paper. Because it is relatively soft, paper does not make a good cutting surface, and sliced and cut-out pieces may have fuzzy edges.

Vinyl is a good surface for modelling, but not for any project that requires cutting. I used a vinyl tablecloth as a work surface for many years, but I cut lots of holes in it and the clay eventually stained it. The texture embellished the bottom surface of many of my projects and now I work on a large ceramic tile with a matte finish.

Unvarnished wood and soft plastic cutting boards are fair work surfaces. Polymer clay will pick up texture from these materials and you may have difficulty in cleaning the clay away from all the nicks and grooves.

Never work on a varnished surface. Plasticizers contained in the clay can damage varnish (even fingernail varnish!). Plastics can also be damaged by plasticizers in polymer clay. If in doubt, don't use it.

Blades ★

Craft blades, single-edged razor blades and even paring knives are adequate for many polymer clay projects. Because these blades are often short and thick, I recommend longer, thinner blades★ that you can find from several sources. Wallpaper scraper replacement blades are available at do-it-yourself stores; medical suppliers carry skin graft blades (also known as tissue blades), which are very sharp and long, and at least two manufacturers now make blades exclusively for use with polymer clay (see Useful Information, page 110). You may well be able to find these in some of the larger craft stores. If mokume gane and millefiori techniques (see pages 20 and 22) are among your plans, do take time to find one of these long, sharp blades.

Designer Sue Heaser (see Further Reading, page 110) recommends using a craft knife with a curved blade★, which she uses for appliqué and mosaic techniques in polymer clay. It is a good all-purpose blade and I found it very useful for cutting out templates and sculpting (see Curious Cat, pages 38–9).

Rolling tools ★

In polymer clay work you often need to make uniform sheets or layers, flatten round logs to make them into square ones and smooth joins. A print roller or brayer★ is fine to use for all these purposes. Art supply stores stock print rollers. If possible, buy an acrylic or lucite roller. Rubber rollers will do, but they are easily nicked and will transfer nick marks onto the clay. If you choose a wooden roller, make sure that it is very smooth.

Pasta Machine

The tool that has saved me the most time is the pasta machine. Besides being useful for quickly rolling uniform layers of clay, it can also condition clay and to blend colours. For techniques such as mokume gane and millefiori (see pages 20 and 22), a pasta machine is well worth the investment. Just glance through this book and see how many projects call for a layer of clay. You will soon realize just how worthwhile a pasta machine can be.

Pasta machine

Piercing tools ★

Beads and buttons need piercing and wool needles★ work admirably. Needle tools give you a little more to hold onto as you work. For large holes, use knitting needles, toothpicks or wooden skewers. These tools are for piercing prior to baking. I prefer to hand-pierce buttons where possible because I can round the edges of the holes.

To pierce clay after baking, use a hobby drill. Drill bits come in a range of sizes, so you'll always be able to find the one that is right for your project. I use a drill press and recommend that you use a jig to hold the bead straight up and down. This is the quickest way to pierce large quantities of beads. As the beads are already cured, their shapes will not distort with this method (see page 18 for further advice).

Ruler ★

Always use a ruler to measure out lengths, diameters and as a cutting guide whenever you need a straight edge. For the projects featured in this book, the ruler should measure in metric units down to millimetres or imperial units down to one-sixteenth of an inch. I prefer to use a wooden ruler to avoid any problems with incompatible plastics.

Modelling, carving & shaping tools

You can choose whether to spend a little or a lot on tools for modelling polymer clay before it is cured (hardened) or for carving it after curing. Visit an art materials store to find linoleum cutters, which are good for cutting and incising. There is a range of commercially available modelling, carving, sculpting, detailing and shaping tools specially made for ease of use and designed for specific types of work. If you find yourself leaning towards figurine- or doll-making or carving, these tools may be a good investment for you.

To save money, look for modelling and carving tools around your home. Sewing boxes, tool boxes, manicure sets and the

kitchen are all good sources for polymer clay tools. Look for items such as knitting needles, old dental tools, pencils, craft blades, pins, toothpicks, a garlic press, wire, cuticle pushers, tracing wheels and stitching tools. If you've decided to give up sugarcraft, you can use those tools for polymer clay crafting, but don't ever use them for sugarcraft again.

Ball stylus The only modelling tool listed in Standard Equipment & Supplies (see page 15) is a ball stylus★ or try a pin with a round head.

A clay gun looks similar to a cookie press, with various shaped discs and sizes of holes. After fitting a disc onto the end of the clay gun, you load soft clay into the barrel and press the plunger. The clay gun extrudes a strand of clay with a cross section that is exactly the same shape as the hole in the disc. Thin, round strands

Modelling, carving & shaping tools

1 Clay gun
2 Discs for clay gun
3 Modelling and
* carving tools*
4 Shaped cutters
5 Small biscuit
* cutters*
6 Clay cutters

make good hair for figurines and, because they are so uniform, the strands can also be combined to make precise millefiori.

Pattern cutters are like tiny biscuit cutters and these are available in many shapes. Some clay cutters have spring-returned plungers to dislodge the cut clay. If you never plan to use them for food again, petits fours cutters and other small biscuit cutters also work well. For realistic leaves, try sugarcraft leaf cutting and veining sets (they cannot be re-used for sugarcraft), or cut clay around real leaves and press the leaves into the clay to "vein" it.

*Texturing tools
with examples*

moulds so that the moulded clay can be easily released.

Baking surface ★

I prefer baking on a ceramic tile. If it is glossy, cover it with clean white paper to avoid a shiny spot appearing where your work touches its surface. Baking trays work well too, but again, line with paper.

To bake beads, some artists suspend them on a skewer or knitting needle with the ends resting on the edges of a baking tray with raised sides.

Oven & potholders ★

Use any conventional oven or toaster oven to cure polymer clay. For best results, use a thermometer to check the oven temperature. First, set the oven to a specific temperature and use the thermometer to determine whether the oven actually heats up to the exact temperature that you require. If not, then adjust the oven setting to achieve the correct temperature.

The curing temperatures suggested by polymer clay manufacturers are for conventional ovens. If you have a fan-assisted oven, read the owner's manual for the appropriate time and temperature adjustments. I recommend testing as above with a thermometer.

Texturing tools

Texturing tools are all around you – for example, toothbrushes, wadded paper, fabric, baskets, screws, stones, seashells and crumpled foil.

A tracing wheel from your sewing box has a serrated edge to press through sewing patterns and tracing paper to transfer marks to the fabric below. Roll the serrated edge on polymer clay for a texture that looks just like stitching. Sugarcrafters use a similar tool known as a stitch wheel. You can also create ornamental and figurative textures with rubber and leather stamps or patterned styluses. Buy them or make your own.

Commercial push-moulds

Moulds

See Techniques, pages 20–1 for advice on making your own push-moulds from polymer clay by using buttons, carvings, seashells, charms and many other objects as originals. Choose from a wide variety of commercially available push-moulds which are sold in craft stores. These are all perfect for repetitive, dimensional, flat-on-the-back work that you do with polymer clay, such as button-making, creating ornaments to glue onto flat surfaces (see the frames on pages 90–1), cabochons or other raised designs for brooches or pendants. Talcum powder is commonly used to dust

*Commercial and home-made push-moulds
with untrimmed and trimmed samples*

Specialist tools

Bear in mind for the future the tools that follow in this section. If you decide to become a prolific polymer clay hobbyist or professional, they will all help you immensely in certain specific areas. The manufacturers are all listed in Useful Information (see page 110).

Marxit®

Invented by Donna Kato, this tool has six ridged sides. The ridges are spaced at 3mm, 5mm, 7mm, 10mm, 15mm and 20mm. (These are the actual markings and inch marks are not provided at all.) Press one side of this tool gently against a millefiori

Marxit tool

cane for example, and it makes marks on the cane at precise intervals. Cut through each mark to make evenly sized slices. This tool can also be used to make uniformly sized or graded beads (see Techniques, page 19).

JASI cane slicer

JASI cane slicer

Invented by Judith Skinner and designed for slicing millefiori canes up to 7.5cm (3in) wide, this tool makes it possible to create slices of uniform thickness and, best of all, individual slices that are the same thickness from top to bottom and from side to side. If you've ever sliced a cane, you will know how difficult it is to keep your blade perfectly perpendicular to the cutting surface. At the cutting edge, braces support wide canes so that you are able to cut very thin (1mm/¹⁄₃₂in) slices of canes.

Buffer

Polymer clay can be sanded and buffed to a high gloss. To do this, use a bench-mounted lathe fitted with a cotton buffing wheel.

Buffing wheel

Blender, food processor or spice mill

You can save your hands by whirling small chunks of clay in a blender, food processor or spice mill to begin the conditioning process. For crumbly clay, some artists add a few drops of mineral oil or diluent. Remember that once you have used a blender, food processor or spice mill for clay, it should never be used again for food.

Supplies

Visit craft, art supply and do-it-yourself stores for most of the supplies you'll need for working with polymer clay. You may already have many of these at home.

Glue ★

Extra-strong glue (often known as "Super Glue") works well on cured or uncured polymer clay. Use it to glue clay pieces together or to other surfaces. Pieces can be baked at clay-curing temperatures. It is available in liquid and gel forms, and with several choices of nozzle shapes.

For fail-proof adhesion, use two-part epoxy. I recommend it for gluing cured polymer clay to glass or metal, such as jewellery findings. It is available in larger craft and do-it-yourself stores. Read and follow the manufacturer's instructions for mixing and using, and always follow the safety advice that they recommend.

Sandpaper ★

Do-it-yourself and hardware stores sell wet/dry sandpaper in various grades. I use the standard sizes which are 240, 400, 600 and 1000, which is very fine. Always sand cured clay under running water to avoid air-borne polymer clay dust.

Paint

Acrylic paint is best for use on polymer clay. Oil paints may react with the cured clay. After painting polymer clay, leave the paint to dry thoroughly, coat the painted

Acrylic paints

Brush-on powders, glitters, pastels, metal leaf & gilding compounds

1 Rub-on gilding compound
2 Brush-on metallic powder
3, 4 and 5 Various glitters
6 Embossing powder

7 Pearlescent powder
8 Metal leaf
9 Brush for applying metal leaf
10 Artist's pastels

piece with glaze. Try a trick from designer Sue Heaser, which gives you the chance to correct painting mistakes: coat the piece first with gloss glaze and leave to dry. If necessary, sketch the design lightly with a pencil, then apply acrylic paint. Should you make a mistake, simply scrape the paint off the piece with a sharp knife or blade. When you are satisfied with the paint job, leave it to dry and then glaze once more.

Paintbrushes

Use paintbrushes to apply paint and glaze to cured polymer clay. These brushes need not be expensive; man-made bristles are fine, but make sure there are no stray bristles. Choose a brush size that is appropriate for the individual project. Size 0000 (also written as 4/0) is a tiny brush that is best for use when painting miniatures and also for fine detailing.

Brush-on powders & glitters

Give polymer clay pieces a pearly or metallic patina using brush-on powder. Brush the powder onto the uncured clay using a paintbrush. After curing, coat the surface with glaze. Eberhard Faber manufactures a line of metallic powders specifically for use with polymer clay. Polymer clay artists also use embossing powders and their metallic effect is achieved with bits of mica (a rock-forming mineral).

Sprinkle glitter onto uncured clay too. After curing, coat the surface with glaze to keep the glitter in place.

Artist's pastels

You can add delicate colour or shading to polymer clay with artist's pastels. Rub the pastel onto paper first to make a fine coloured powder, then use a paintbrush to apply the powder to uncured polymer clay. Bake the clay and then coat it with glaze to seal the powder.

Artist's pastels are a particularly messy material. Clean your hands and work area thoroughly after use.

Metal leaf & gilding compounds

Metal leaf now goes beyond the traditional gold, silver and copper varieties into multicolour and patterned leaves. Applied to uncured clay, it can be rolled out for a crackle effect. It is often used in mokume gane (see page 20).

Apply metallic gilding compounds with a fingertip and then buff with a soft cloth. Do not use them for items that will be heavily used or worn.

Herbs, spices, sand & more

Mix dry materials with polymer clay for a number of attractive effects. Polymer clay artist Sue Heaser mixes semolina with clay to make realistically-textured miniature breads and cake. Pepper and herbs, too can also look very convincing. Make sure that the materials you use are dry, so that they won't be subject to mildew or rot.

Glazes

The glazes designed specifically for polymer clay come in matte and gloss formulations, and are water- or solvent-based. I prefer to buy the smaller bottles that are fitted with brushes and decant from larger jars. Use glazes, especially the solvent-based varieties, in a well-ventilated area.

Acrylic-based floor wax gives a delicate sheen to sanded polymer clay. You can also use spray-on acrylic artist's glazes, but try the glaze out on a test piece first to ensure that it is compatible with polymer clay.

Mineral oil or diluent

A few drops of mineral oil or a specially-formulated diluent (Polyform Products manufacture Sculpey Diluent) revives crumbly clay. The diluent is a plasticizer.

Glazes

Before you begin

Save time by gathering all the necessary supplies and tools before you start work on any project.

Templates

Many of the projects in this book use templates and these are provided with the making-up instructions. Trace full-size templates, or photocopy at 100 per cent. Templates in this book are actual size unless otherwise stated. To enlarge, photocopy as instructed on the templates. For simple shapes where the directions give only the dimensions, measure and draw the shape out on paper first, then cut out the drawing and use it as a template.

For a cut-out template, first cut the template out of paper, lay it over the clay and use a craft knife to cut around it. Remove the excess clay and the template, then neaten the cut edges.

To trace a template, lay the template over the clay. Lightly trace the indicated lines using a pencil or craft knife. This transfers the lines to the clay.

You can use household items, such as cup and bowl rims, film canisters, biscuit cutters, plates and lids, to make circular templates in a variety of sizes. Just trace the outline out onto paper first, then cut the circle carefully out of the paper and use this as your template.

Standard equipment & supplies

The instructions in this book list all the materials that you will need to make the projects and the list on this page contains the tools and supplies that are used most frequently in this book. It is also a good basic list for a beginner. In the project materials listings, I continually refer to this list as "Standard equipment and supplies". For further information, refer to the previous sections in this book on Equipment and Supplies (see pages 8–15 and refer to the photograph and key on page 9).

STANDARD EQUIPMENT & SUPPLIES
- Working surface (please include at least one ceramic tile)
- Baking surface
- Rolling equipment
- Craft knife with curved blade
- Long, thin blade
- Wool and darning needles or needle tools
- Ball stylus or round-headed pin
- Clean, white copier paper
- Pencil
- Scissors
- Ruler
- Glue
- Wet/dry sandpaper in a range of 240, 400, 600 and 1000 (optional) grade sizes

Working with polymer clay

As you work wtih polymer clay, the processes and precautions described below will become second nature to you.

Conditioning

To make polymer clay pliable enough to work with, roll and press it between your hands and then fold the clay. Repeat until it is soft and pliable.

Different clays condition differently. Conditioning time varies according to the brand, different colours of the same brand, the age of the clay, your body heat and the room temperature. Buy fresh clay and look for dates or coded dates on clay wrappers. Use your clay within a year of purchase and store in a cool place.

Prewarming clay sometimes helps in conditioning it. Some clays, such as Sculpey Super-Flex, require prewarming. You can sit on a clay package or tuck it under your arm and this may help to warm it. If you warm clay by placing it under a warm lightbulb or in a sunny spot, you must be particularly watchful so that you prevent your clay from curing and becoming permanently hard, and take all sensible safety precautions.

If you find that your clay is very stiff, break it down into small chunks. Condition one chunk, then add another and condition again. Repeat until all the chunks are conditioned. You may also need a softening compound (see Materials, page 8).

A pasta machine on its widest setting can also be used for conditioning some clays directly from the package. Some clays need to be preconditioned first. Cold machines can cool the clay. If the room is cold, place an adjustable lamp next to the machine, position the light bulb so that it is about 15cm (6in) above the machine and turn on the lamp.

People who use a lot of polymer clay invest in blenders or food processors (see page 13) to help condition clay. To do this, break the clay up into chunks, place it in the container or bowl and chop it by pulsing the blade. You can add a few drops of mineral oil or diluent if the clay is very dry.

Curing polymer clay

Always check the wrapper to confirm the baking time and temperature for polymer clay. For the most part, the clays used in this book are baked at 130°C (250°F/Gas ½) for 20 minutes, although some of the manufacturers recommend baking times that depend on thickness. FIMO Art Translucent and so-called Flesh colours bake at 100°C (212°F/Gas ⅛). These clays discolour or plaque if they are baked at too hot a temperature (see Troubleshooting, pages 18–19).

I haven't come across any adverse effects from baking clay for longer than recommended. Heat takes longer to penetrate large pieces so a longer baking time ensures that even the centre of a large piece eventually heats up to the correct temperature for curing.

Quenching

Strengthen cured polymer clay by plunging it into cold water immediately after curing. This method, which is known as quenching, was pioneered by

doll-maker Linda Struble. She uses FIMO-brand polymer clay and cures it at 130°C (250°F/Gas ½) for one hour and this is longer than the recommended 20 minutes. Linda then bakes it for another half an hour after reducing the temperature to 115°C (240°F/Gas ¼). As soon as she takes the cured clay from the oven, she puts it into cold tap water. Clay treated in this way is much more flexible.

Leeching

To stiffen a very soft clay, you can soak some of the plasticizer out of the clay through a process known as leeching. To do this, first break the clay up into chunks and place them on a sheet of white paper (or between two sheets of paper if you're in a hurry). Then leave the clay for a couple of hours. As the plasticizer starts to soak into the paper from the clay, you will find that greasy-looking spots will begin to appear. Once the spots appear, remember to check the clay at regular intervals. As soon as the consistency of the clay is right, remove it from the paper. If you accidentally leave the clay on the paper for too long, it will become crumbly in texture.

> **SAFETY NOTE**
>
> Burned or charred polymer clay produces dangerous fumes. If you accidentally burn polymer clay, turn the oven off, use oven gloves to take the burned clay out of the building, then ventilate the kitchen and stay away until the fumes dissipate. Wrap the cooled clay in newspaper and dispose of it carefully.
>
> Never quench a polymer clay project that contains glass. The rapid change in temperature may cause the glass to crack.

Rolling techniques

Use your hands to roll clay into long, thin snakes or short, fat logs. Roll gently for a smoother log. To reduce the diameter of a log or snake, place your hands at the centre of its length, then roll as you move your hands away from the centre.

Try to cup your hands as you roll a ball of clay for the roundest results. If you should pull your fingers back and flatten your palms, the ball of clay will take on a bicone shape.

To shape a log of clay into a square length, place it on the work surface. Roll the brayer gently along the top to flatten it so that the log is slightly flattened on the top and bottom, and the sides bulge. Now turn the log over to its side and roll again with the brayer. Turn and roll until the log is square.

For a triangular length, place the log on a work surface. Holding the brayer at a 60° angle to the work surface, roll it to flatten the side at an angle. Turn the flattened side down and roll at an angle again. Turn and roll for a triangular cane.

Use a brayer to smooth joins, for example when you wrap canes or join the edges of clay sheets. When stacking layers of clay together, roll the brayer over the top to press out air bubbles.

Specific thicknesses

Many of the projects in this book require layers or sheets of polymer clay in specific thicknesses. Hobby and model stores supply wood in the correct thicknesses that you can use as a guide: tape two wood lengths onto your work surface, just far enough apart so that the ends of your rolling tool rest on the edges of the wood strips. Put the clay that is to be rolled between the wood strips and roll it down until the roller rests on the edges of the strips. The clay between the strips will be the same thickness as the strips.

Using a pasta machine

A pasta machine allows you to roll uniformly thick layers of clay relatively quickly. For best results, try to have a

GUIDE TO THINNESS OF LAYERS ACHIEVED WITH A PASTA MACHINE

Pasta machine setting (Atlas Queen®)	Approx. mm	Approx. fraction of an inch	Rounded measurements
1	2.6	.1	3mm (⅛in)
2	2.5	.098	2.5mm (⅒in)
3	2.2	.087	n/a
4	1.6-1.7	.065	1.5mm (⅟₁₆in)
5	1.1	.044	1mm (⅟₃₂in)
6	0.6	.025	0.5mm (⅟₆₄in)
7	0.01	.001	paper-thin

warm pasta machine and condition the clay (see pages 15–16) well. If the clay crumbles as you roll it through, condition it again. Soft, easy-to-condition clays tend to tear or blister at very thin pasta machine settings, whereas the stiffer clays roll beautifully to paper-thinness.

Begin rolling the clay through the pasta machine at its widest setting. For thinner sheets, reduce the width between rollers, one setting at a time, rolling after each setting change until the sheet is the required thickness.

I often get oddly shaped clay sheets with the first pass through the machine. However, I fold the shape in half, cut off the pieces that stick out, then patch them into the places that don't have quite enough clay and roll again. A few passes through the machine gives me a piece with fairly straight edges. If the edges crack, fold them to the inside before rolling again.

The Atlas Queen® pasta machine seems to be favoured among clay users. It comes with a cutter that is normally used for fettucine but you can use this to cut clay strips and it works best with stiffer clays. The table above will give you an idea of how thin a layer the pasta machine can make (the layers were measured with calipers). Measurements will naturally vary according to individual machines, clay brands and the degree of handling. The samples I used for testing the layers were all made of FIMO-Silver polymer clay.

Cutting polymer clay

Use a craft knife (see blades★, page 10) to cut around templates, trim or cut using a straight edge, to divide up blocks of clay and for most of the other small cutting jobs. For millefiori canes and mokume gane assemblies, use a long thin blade, which is also useful for cutting pieces that are wider than the length of a craft knife.

To minimize distortion when cutting round logs or canes, roll the cane as you slice. This more-or-less equalizes the pressure around pieces as you cut, so the slices stay rounder. For this to work, you must hold your blade perpendicular to the work surface.

To slice logs or canes that are not round, hold the blade perpendicular to the work surface and press the cutting edge straight down in one movement. Even with the thinnest blade, the pierce will distort to some degree. Turn the log to a different side for each cut to minimize any distortion. If the log is very soft, refrigerate it or leave it to rest before you cut it.

Safety note: To avoid any accidents, be careful to look at your blade first before you pick it up and make sure that you always pick it up from the notched or holey edge.

Covering objects with polymer clay

The curing temperature for polymer clay is low enough so that it won't damage glass, metal, eggshells and most types of wood. These materials can all be covered decoratively with polymer clay. Wash glass and metal objects that are to be covered thoroughly, wipe them with methylated spirits and leave to dry. Always wash eggs first before you blow them out, then rinse them well afterwards and then leave to dry. Before covering wood, bake it for 30–45 minutes at 130°C (250°F/Gas ½), then leave it to cool. This dries out the moisture and exposes cracks in the wood, which you may then fill in with polymer clay. If wood is not prebaked, then moisture can cause bubbles in the clay.

If your decorative clay is to be pressed directly onto the surface, cover the jar, box, frame, egg, cutlery handle (or whatever) first with a thin layer of plain or scrap polymer clay. Roll it with a brayer or between your hands to smooth and press out any air bubbles, then find an inconspicuous spot to pierce one or more small holes in the clay cover. I prefer to bake at this point; you must experiment to find your preference. Next, apply decorative slices or layers onto the scrap layer. Roll again to smooth and press out the bubbles. Bake, cool and sand under running water.

When the design is such that you can't use a scrap layer, make your decorative cover at least 3mm (⅛in) thick. This allows you to sand the cured clay and small air pockets won't be strong enough to cause bubbles in the clay.

Cleaning & cleaning up

Before you begin working with polymer clay, make sure that your hands and work surfaces are clean especially before using translucent, doll skin colours or glow-in-the-dark clays.

When you do pick up a wayward bit of polymer clay, try to catch it while it's still just on the surface of the project. You can then cut away tiny slices, minimizing the loss of project clay, until the spot is gone. Polymer clay residue can be cleaned from your hands with a few drops of baby or vegetable oil. Rub the oil into the residue, then wash with soap and water.

Sanding & polishing

Cured polymer clay sands to a silky smooth finish. Smooth your clay as much as possible before baking. After baking, begin sanding under a gently running tap with 240-grade size wet/dry sandpaper. When the surface feels smooth to the touch, move up to 400-grade and sand all around. Repeat with 600-grade sandpaper and, if you can find it, 1000-grade sandpaper. Rinse the project and dry it. Polish with a cotton cloth or a piece of quilting wadding.

After sanding, you can paint or spray the piece with glaze or polish it with acrylic wax. You can buff and polish polymer clay by mechanical means to a satin-like sheen or a high gloss. Polishing by hand takes some time, but it can be done with a cotton cloth. For quicker results, use a drill or bench-mounted lathe fitted with a cotton buffing wheel

(see page 13) or a rubber wheel covered with a sheepswool polishing bonnet. As the wheel turns, hold the project so that the threads of the frayed cotton wheel hit it. If you are using sheepswool, hold the project to the edge of the wheel so that just the fibres hit it. Move the project around slowly to ensure all the surfaces are evenly polished.

If you hold a project too close to the buffing wheel, it may grind a groove in the project. Stop and sand away the groove, then go back to polishing.

Piercing polymer clay

Hand-piercing beads and buttons needs to be done before baking using a wool needle, skewer, toothpick, knitting needle or a professional needle-tool. For the least distortion of the piece, pierce from one side until the needle's point is just visible on the other side of the bead. Remove the needle and pierce from the other side, twirling it to enlarge the hole as needed.

I recommend a hobby drill mounted to a drill press for piercing. Select the bit size that is appropriate for your project and install it. Hold the piece by hand or in a jig. Press down on the drill press handle. The drill will throw up plastic strands which twist around the top of the bit. Stop from time to time, allow the plastic to cool and pull it off the drill bit.

Safety precautions

When working with polymer clay, be sensible and take all the recommended safety precautions, pay careful attention to what you are doing, plan ahead and this will save you time, money and possibly your health in the long run. Make sure that you always read and follow the manufacturer's instructions, which are printed on the product labels. If you decide to deviate from these, do so with extreme caution and be prepared to act if anything goes wrong.

I've said these things before, but they bear repeating: always look before you pick up any blade to make sure you take it

from the notched or holey edge, and before you bake, always check that the oven settings are correct. Too-high temperatures will char creations and release dangerous fumes (see page 16). If you notice a strong chemical odour or the smell of burning, turn off the oven immediately. Does your clay seem as though it is melting or is it burned? If so, use heatproof gloves to take it outside immediately. Ventilate the room, then leave it, taking other people and animals with you, and don't come back until the fumes are gone.

Always sand polymer clay under running water. It isn't good to breathe in the tiny plastic particles that sanding releases. When you machine buff or polish polymer clay, always wear a dust mask to avoid breathing in the dust and I also recommend safety glasses when buffing or drilling.

When used with care, metallic and embossing powders are perfectly safe. If you are sensitive to airborne particles, please wear a dust mask whenever you use these products. Use polymer clay glazes in a well-ventilated area.

Polymer clay enters a stage that is known as "gelation" (between 55°C and 80°C/130°F and 180°F) before it begins to harden permanently. With this in mind, consider the climate in which you live. Is it warm or hot? Don't leave fresh polymer clay in a hot, parked car or in hot spots around your home.

Don't stored uncured clay wrapped in a porous material such as paper. It will leech (see page 16) the plasticizer away from the clay until it eventually becomes unworkable. Polymer clay colours will fade if they are exposed to bright sunlight. Store uncured clay in a cool, dark place and keep finished projects away from bright, sunny areas.

Troubleshooting

Crumbly clay is either old or it has been stored incorrectly. Revive old clay by adding softeners (see Materials, page 8)

SAFETY NOTE

Pay particular attention while sanding to avoid sanding the skin off your fingertips or sanding away your fingernails. When machine buffing, wear a dust mask to avoid breathing in fine polymer clay particles. Do your buffing away from food preparation areas and unmasked people.

Wear safety glasses while drilling to protect your eyes. Clean up tiny bits of plastic from your work area after drilling, especially if you have children or animals around the house.

How to store opened clay

or add a few drops of mineral oil or diluent. With time and lots of kneading, you can revive old clay. To avoid this problem, buy fresh clay. Some clays have dates printed on the package, while others are coded. For example, the code on FIMO brand clay is a letter which represents the month (A is January, and so on) and a number which is the last digit of the year (8 is 1998). Try to use polymer clay within a year of buying it. Store opened packages in plastic bags with zip enclosures in a cool, dark place.

Whenever you see plaquing or bubbles in the surface of cured clay, inadequate conditioning may be the culprit. Plaquing is the appearance of pale, almost circular marks on the baked clay which cannot be sanded away. Some clays are so pliable immediately they are removed from the package that you are tempted to use them without conditioning. However, resist the urge and condition first. Designer Donna Kato refers to a point in conditioning soft clays such as Sculpey, where the feel of the clay changes which indicates that it has been conditioned enough. You will learn to recognize this point with experience.

Plaquing occurs in some clays when you bake them at too hot a temperature. Always check the package for the curing

temperature. Keep your curing clay in the centre of the oven away from the heating elements. Always check the package for the correct curing temperature; some transparent and translucent clays cure several degrees cooler than others. For important pieces, you could even bake a test piece of clay first and adjust the temperature if necessary.

Thin and protruding pieces can slump during curing. Support these pieces with wadded or folded paper or foil. You will find that thin layers of sheets of polymer clay, such as plaques, sometimes warp during or after curing. Avoid warping by first covering the polymer clay piece with a sheet of paper and weight it with a ceramic tile during curing and cooling. A cured piece that crumbles or breaks easily has not been cured at the correct temperature. Calibrate your oven (see the advice on oven temperatures in Tools, page 12).

If a piece breaks cleanly, glue it back together carefully with extra-strong glue. For breaks where pieces are missing, glue together the pieces you can, fill in the remaining gaps with the appropriate colour of polymer clay and bake for about five minutes. Make sure that you support any thin or protruding pieces and then sand to smooth.

Techniques

Don't be afraid to experiment and add your own techniques to the following list.

Mixing colours & clays
Different brands of polymer clay can be used together in one project. However, we don't know the long-term effects of mixing brands. To increase the chance that your work will stand the test of time, it's probably best to take the most cautious route of using just the one brand of clay in one project.

Polymer clay offers an unlimited palette through colour mixing. Cut clay blocks into uniform chunks and mix small quantities until you get the shade you require. Try to keep track of your colour formulations in a notebook, preferably with sample colour chips.

Small amounts of strong, dark colours, such as red, black and navy, can change the lighter colours drastically. Adding translucent to a colour gives it depth, while fluorescent colours lend a subtle glow when they are mixed with their non-fluorescent counterparts.

Uniform & graduated bead or button sizes
Make a snake of clay which is uniformly thick across its length. To make beads that are all the same size, cut the same length of snake for each bead.

To make graduated sizes of beads or buttons, roll a snake as before and use a rule and a blade or the Marxit tool (see Tools, page 13) to mark intervals of, say, 3mm (⅛in) along the length of the snake. Slice the cane at 3mm (⅛in) intervals for the smallest beads. For the next size up, include two marked intervals (6mm/¼in) in each slice. The next size up is three intervals, and so on.

Making a hanger
Cut a 10cm (4in) length of picture wire. Twist the ends together to form a loop. Using no more than one quarter block of polymer clay, cover the twisted ends and about half of the wire loop with clay.

Candy cane twist

Shape the clay into a rough rectangle. For a light piece, such as the name plaques on pages 72–5, flatten the clay to about 7mm (¼in). Use your judgement for other, heavier projects and flatten the clay rectangle appropriately. Bake for 20 minutes, then glue it to the back of the project with two-part epoxy.

Making a candy cane twist
Begin with two (or more) snakes of clay, about 5cm (2in) long. Twist them together and roll to smooth. Holding one end gently on the work surface, roll the other end backwards or forwards across the surface to continue the twist. Roll and twist and gently reduce the twist as you roll (see Rolling, page 16), breaking the length to keep it manageable. Continue until you are pleased with the diameter and degree of twist.

If you intend to apply the twist to another surface and to smooth it, bear in mind that it will fatten as it flattens, so make the twist thinner than you want it to look on the finished product.

Making wood grain
Begin with a log of the main wood colour (usually a shade of brown– see opposite). Make thin snakes of the grain colours and cut two or three pieces of each that are the same length as the main colour log. Place them along the length of the log so that they are evenly spaced all around and roll to smooth. Then fold the log in half or thirds and roll again. Continue folding and rolling until the grain is as you like it.

If you need to make several batches of wood grain, count the number of times you fold the log and make a note of it so that you can repeat the effect exactly.

Try mixing the main wood colour with an equal amount of translucent (adjust the baking temperature accordingly) to give it a little depth. I like to use one grain colour that is lighter than the main one and one that is darker.

Mokume gane
In mokume gane, polymer clay borrows from a metalworking technique from Japan. Begin with a stack of polymer clay sheets. Crumble, fold or poke little hills into this polymer clay sandwich. Slice the tops of the peaks that you have created using a long, thin blade. Carefully flatten the cut piece with a brayer and the result looks like a map.

The most delicate look is achieved by using layers of translucent and tinted translucent clay which are separated by sheets of metal leaf. The example shown above uses translucent clay, translucent clay tinted with transparent pink and a pink and gold swirl patterned metal leaf. Translucent clay allows the metal leaf to shine through. In the photograph you can see the original polymer clay sandwich, the poked and prodded sandwich and two versions of the sliced and flattened sandwich. The tops that you slice off the peaks are pretty, too. While they are still on your blade, slap them down onto a plain layer of clay and flatten it. The other two pieces shown are cut-off tops which have been applied to a plain layer of clay.

Mokume gane

Making moulds & casting
To make a mould, use a soft polymer clay. Make a ball of clay that is big enough to spread beyond the edges of the object that you are using to make the mould. Generously sprinkle the top of the clay ball with talcum powder and press the object firmly into the clay until the clay rises to the widest level of the object. Take the object out of the clay and bake the resulting mould for 20 minutes.

Wood grain

To make casts, sprinkle the mould with talcum powder and tap out the excess. For a deep mould, use a little more clay than is required to fill the mould and form it into a raindrop shape that is narrower than the edges of the design to be cast. With the point down, press the clay into the mould. Fill the impression up to its edges with clay. Use the excess clay as a handle to pull or wiggle the clay from the mould and trim away the extra clay.

For a shallow mould, dust with talcum powder as before. Press a ball of clay into the impression to fill it to its edges. Carefully tease the clay from the edge and pull it out of the mould. If necessary, trim away excess clay from the edges or back of the mould and smooth any cut edges on the cast. If you plan to glue the cast onto a flat surface, sand the back gently after baking.

Using metal leaf

A fat brush is made for the purpose of lifting sheetings of metal leaf and smoothing them onto your uncured polymer clay. For a crackle effect, cover a sheet of polymer clay with metal leaf. Roll the polymer clay more thinly with a brayer or pasta machine. As the clay expands underneath, the metal leaf cracks and leaves long, thin pieces of metal in the clay. If you turn the clay sheet a quarter turn and roll again, the cracked metal pieces will be closer to square shapes. Coat the cured polymer clay with glaze to seal the metal leaf.

Metal leaf

The Skinner technique

Designer Judith Skinner developed an exciting technique that allows you to make subtle colour gradations in clay without batch mixing. With a pasta machine, this happens very quickly. To shade a piece from turquoise to gold, construct a square or rectangle with turquoise and gold sheets (measuring about 3mm/⅛in thick) joined along a diagonal as shown here. Fold the piece in half with the two-colour ends together, then put the folded edge first into the pasta machine and roll down to 3mm (⅛in) thick again. Fold in the same direction, tap the edges of the resulting rectangle on your work surface to even them up, and roll again. Continue folding, squaring up and rolling until you see a good gradation between colours at the ends.

Set the pasta machine to very thin (about 0.5mm/¹⁄₆₄in). Turn the piece a quarter turn, feeding a solid colour end into the pasta machine and roll the piece through. You now have a long, thin piece that grades between two colours. If you roll it from one end, you'll have a log with a cross section which grades from one colour in the middle to the other colour around the outside. Fold it accordion-style for a squared cane that grades from one colour at the bottom to the other colour at the top.

The photograph shows two rolled canes and a bead embellished with slices of one of the canes. The pink and black piece was made from a graded strip folded accordion-style and then cut and stacked to move back and forth between black and pink. Shaded bits add dimension to millefiori (see Ladybird Light Switch, pages 92–3).

This process is not limited to two colours. Add

Skinner technique samples

as many slanted pieces of colour as you care to or as will fit through your pasta machine. The colours at the ends should be squared off.

Anderson's clay gun wrapping technique

Designer Ester Anderson discovered that she could achieve the effect of a wrapped clay log by using a correctly loaded clay gun. Here, I will use the colours red and white to explain this technique. First, load a slug of red clay into the clay gun (about one-eighth of a block is the right amount). Right behind the red, load the same amount of white and press the plunger to extrude a strand of clay.

The outside of the strand is red and inside, a white core creeps into the red. As the white core becomes larger, the red walls start to thin. By the time all the clay is pushed out, the red walls may be so thin that you can see the white shining through. Use the extruded strands for making millefiori, or you could cut cross sections of strands and use them as delicate tiles (see Tesserae Bangles, pages 48–9).

Millefiori

The term "millefiori" has become a general phrase to describe any construction of clay (usually called a "cane"), where the design element is found in the cross section. Tiled Nightlight Holders (see page 62–3), Tiled Cutlery (pages 80–1) and the Victorian Fireplace tiles (see pages 34–7) are a few of the designs in this book that use this technique.

We are fortunate enough to be able to buy pre-made, uncured millefiori canes to use for bead-making and decoratively covering objects. These canes are about 5cm (2in) long and are available in a range of different designs, including seasonal motifs.

Two words commonly used to describe polymer clay millefiori are "cane" and "reduce". A cane is a construction whose cross section contains a design. To reduce is to make a cane smaller by pressing and stretching it. Reduce round canes by gently pressing and moving your hands from the middle of the cane to the ends as you roll. Square and other straight-edged canes can be reduced by rolling and pressing gently with a brayer or by pinching and pressing with your fingers.

As you reduce canes, the ends tend to distort because the outside of the cane reduces more quickly than the centre. The outer layers grow over the cane ends, covering the centre and moving ever outwards. Trim the ends until you see the entire design in the cross section. Distortion such as this wastes both clay and time by reducing the usable portions of the cane. One way to avoid this is to reduce gently, stopping at frequent intervals to tap the ends of the cane on your work surface to keep them flat. The other way is to press hard at the middle of the cane's length as you reduce it. Although the ends of the cane will flare out, you will find that a larger portion of the cane will be usable.

The fun of millefiori is to work out how to build the cane so that you get the design you want in the cross section. Among the easiest designs to make are the nine-patch square and the Swiss roll (sometimes referred to as a "jelly roll") (see below).

Making a nine-patch square

Make the same diameter snakes of two clay colours. Cut four pieces of one colour (blue in the photograph), all the same length. Put white, blue and white (for example) next to one another, with their long sides touching. On top of these, stack blue, white and blue in the same direction. Finally, stack white, blue and white. Look at one end and you will see that you have a three-by-three snake square in alternating colours. Press the snakes together, preserving the square shape of the cane and reduce the cane, if desired. Finally, trim the ends. Look for the simple nine-patch design on the large buttons (see page 54). You can use more than two colours in a nine-patch square.

Making a Swiss roll

Stack one thin layer of clay onto another, then taper two opposite edges by pressing or cutting. Beginning at one tapered edge, roll the layers up and reduce, if desired. Trim the ends to see the design better. The roses on the Rosy Bathroom Jar (see pages 84–5) and the scales of one of the Fantasy Fish (see page 59) are Swiss rolls. You can use more than two layers and vary the layers by alternating strips, for instance.

Reducing, stacking & wrapping

The word "millefiori" means "thousand flowers" but it does not necessarily imply a thousand different flowers. It could be just one flower a thousand times, and this is an important characteristic of millefiori. I will illustrate this by using the flower cane from the Victorian Fireplace (see page 35).

All the pieces in the photograph were made using one length of flower cane measuring about 10cm (4in) long. First, I reduced a bit of cane from about 17mm (¾in) to only 5mm (³⁄₁₆in) square. The flower design is intact, only a lot smaller. I then chopped another part of the cane into four pieces and stacked the pieces back together.

I wrapped the four-patch square with another layer of turquoise clay, chopped it into four and stacked the pieces to make a four-patch of four patches. A 7mm (¼in) slice of this makes a large, flat, square bead. I then covered a core of scrap clay with thinner slices and made a barrel bead from this. This is exactly the sort of look that inspired the name "millefiori".

Repeating elements

When you begin to recognize and use repeating elements in your designs, millefiori-making becomes much more efficient. In the nine-patch square, for instance, you don't need to make nine little snakes. You can make two snakes and then chop them into nine pieces.

Nine-patch square

Swiss roll

Millefiori samples

With more experience, you will begin to look for ways to save yourself time by using one cane of polymer clay in several different ways.

Lines in millefiori
A line in a millefiori design is almost always a wrap or an insertion. The turquoise lines between the four-patches in the flower example above (as you know) are wraps. When you surround a cane or log of clay with another colour, it appears as an outline in cross section.

Some lines are the result of cutting a cane lengthwise and inserting a layer of clay. The division between the wing cases of the ladybirds (see Ladybird Light Switch, pages 92–3) is inserted. In the tiles in Victorian Fireplace (see pages 34–7), the line that forms the vein in the leaves is inserted. See if you can recognize an insertion and a wrap in Tiled Night-light Holders (pages 62–3).

Making mosaics in polymer clay
You will need a curved craft knife to make a mosaic with uncured polymer clay tiles. This technique was developed by designer Sue Heaser and the Sun & Sea Wall Clock (see pages 86–9) is a good example of making mosaics. You can make a base for the mosaic by covering an object, such as a lid or brooch back, with uncured clay or by placing a layer of uncured clay on a ceramic tile. This means you won't move it until it is covered with tiles and baked. Trace or mark the lines of the mosaic design on the uncured clay base. The clay base will show between the tiles in the same way that grout does in a traditional mosaic, so choose the colour accordingly.

Make 3mm (⅛in) sheets of the clay that you will use for tiles. Cut strips of clay a little thinner than the desired tile width. As you are working with uncured clay, it will flatten and fatten slightly as you cut, which is why the strips should be narrower than the final width.

To cut and layer the tiles with the curved craft knife, cut a slice about 3mm (⅛in) wide from a strip of clay and lift it with the craft knife. Place the tile on the uncured clay base with the knife and press it into place. If the tile falls off the knife too soon, just cut another one to use. When the base is covered with tiles, press them gently with your hand. Don't squash them, because the edges should be sharp. Bake the tiles as directed on the manufacturer's package.

The Tesserae Bangles (see pages 48–9) and Mother's Day Cards (pages 104–5) are examples of mosaics using cured polymer clay tiles. To make the tiles, roll or pinch lengths of clay to the correct shape or use the clay gun to make clay lengths. Bake these lengths on a ceramic tile for about 5 minutes, then remove the tile from the oven and place it on a hot pad. While the clay is still warm, carefully cut the lightly cured lengths up into 3mm (⅛in) slices.

Make a base of uncured clay as above. Use tweezers to pick up the clay tiles and place them on the base. Press them into the base clay with your finger and bake as directed on the package. Sand if desired or if there are whitish cut-marks on the tiles.

Learning more about polymer clay

Every expert in this world started out as a beginner. You too will become an expert, if you practise long enough. However, you don't have to be one to make beautiful polymer clay pieces. Practice doesn't always mean you learn how. Now and then, you learn what not to do next time. Many of the warnings in this book come directly from my own experience.

Practice is best, but there is a quicker way to learn – from the experts. Read the books that I have listed in Further Reading (see page 110) and join a polymer clay guild. I've learned a lot from reading our excellent British Polymer Clay Guild newsletters and you will too from your local guild's publications. Guilds and other groups sponsor polymer clay workshops. Save money so that you can attend workshops as there is no substitute for learning from someone else in person (see Useful Information, page 110).

For the latest polymer clay news, turn to the internet. Newsgroups offer a wealth of information on techniques, products and people. Sometimes you can read reviews within a few hours after a workshop or other event. Web pages, with their galleries of fine polymer clay work, are very inspirational.

Have a wonderful time experimenting and playing with polymer clay.

Tesserae bangles

2

miniature world

Art Deco-inspired teaset

This Art Deco-style teaset will brighten up any doll's house. Sue Heaser's ingenuity is behind the method for making the saucers and dessert plates. Try different clay colours and patterns to make one-of-a-kind china for your doll's house.

Materials & equipment:

- Standard equipment and supplies (see pages 9 and 15)
- White polymer clay block
- Short wooden dowel, sanded very smoothly at one end, in each of the following diameters: 6mm (¼in) for cups (A), 8mm (⁵⁄₁₆in) for saucers (B) and 10mm (⅜in) for dessert plates (C)
- Talcum powder
- Sheet of acetate, 7.5cm (3in) square
- Gloss glaze
- Black, red and green acrylic paints
- Artist's paintbrush, size 0000

1 Lay the two sugar bowl templates on a 3mm (⅛in) layer of white and cut out the shapes (see page 15). Press the pieces together and smooth the join gently. Repeat for the creamer and pinch the end of the spout to make it slightly pointed. Insert a darning needle into the spout top and drag it outwards slightly to make a hole in the spout. Smooth any rough or uneven spots, then bake for 10 minutes.

2 Next, cut two pieces measuring 4.5 x 6mm (³⁄₁₆ x ¼in) from a 1.5mm (¹⁄₁₆in) layer of white. Place them on the tops of the sugar bowl and creamer as lids (see photograph). Roll two x 1.5mm (¹⁄₁₆in) diameter balls and press one to the middle of each lid. Then roll two x 3mm (⅛in diameter balls and press the bottom of the sugar bowl into a ball so that it flattens and forms a base for the bowl. Repeat to form a base for the creamer. Bake both pieces for 10 minutes.

3 Cut one full teapot template and two teapot templates without the handle and spout from a 3mm (⅛in) layer of white. Cut out the middle of the handle and sandwich the first cut-out between the other two; gently smooth the joins. Smooth the handle, make a hole in the spout and bake for 10 minutes.

4 Then cut a piece measuring 6 x 9mm (¼ x ⅜in) from a 1.5mm (¹⁄₁₆in) layer of white. Place this on top of the teapot for the lid (see main photograph). Roll a 3mm (⅛in) diameter ball and press this in place for the knob on the lid. Then roll a 6mm (¼in) diameter ball and press the bottom of the teapot into the ball as for the sugar bowl above. Bake the assembly for 10 minutes.

5 For each cup, roll a 6mm (¼in) diameter ball. Dust the ball and dowel end A with talcum powder, then press the dowel end into the clay. Press and form the clay up the dowel until the edges are about 6mm (¼in) high or trim to that height, if necessary. Gently remove the cup from the dowel.Cut a strip 1.5mm (¹⁄₁₆in) wide from a 1.5mm (¹⁄₁₆in) layer of white and cut a triangle from this. Place a drop of glue on one triangle edge and glue it to the cup side for a handle (see photograph for guidance). Make as many cups as you need and bake for 10 minutes.

| Teapot | Sugar bowl | Creamer | Cup | Saucer | Dessert plate |

6 For each saucer, cut a 6mm (¼in) length from a 6mm (¼in) diameter clay snake and roll it into a ball. Cover the saucer template with the acetate piece. Put the clay ball on the acetate in the middle of the template and flatten it until it reaches the inner circle edge. Thin the clay out until it reaches the outer circle edge, forming a shallow dome. Sprinkle the dome with talcum powder and sprinkle the cutting edge of a long, thin blade with talcum powder; cut the clay dome away from the acetate with the powdered edge of the blade. Turn the dome over onto a piece of clean white paper or directly onto a ceramic tile for baking. Centre the edge of dowel B over the clay circle and press it gently into the clay until the clay edge pulls up; remove the dowel. Rub your finger gently around

the raised edge to make it even; flatten a little, if necessary, to resemble a saucer rim. Make as many saucers as you need and bake for 10 minutes.

7 To make the dessert plates, cut a 12mm (½in) length from a 6mm (¼in) diameter clay snake. Proceed as for the saucer in Step 6, using dowel C to press up the rim and bake for 10 minutes.

8 Gently sand away imperfections on the teaset and sand the rims of the cups. Coat each piece with gloss glaze and leave to dry. Outline simple flower and leaf shapes in pencil on each piece (refer to main photograph), if desired. Then outline the shapes with black acrylic paint and paint black dots (see photograph). Leave to dry, then fill in the

flowers with red paint and the leaves with green. Leave to dry, then coat with another coat of gloss glaze and leave to dry.

Note:
If you feel discouraged by the imperfections of your dishes, just remember that you are working on 1:12 scale pieces with 1:1 scale fingers and looking at them with 1:1 scale eyes! When this little teaset is nicely laid out on your doll's house table, it will look so much better. A coat of glaze will do wonders, too.

Clockwise from top left: *Teapot, creamer and sugar bowl, the complete teaset, and cup and saucer with matching dessert plate.*

grandfather clock

Inspired by an 18th-century long-case clock, this tall grandfather clock will be a timeless addition to your doll's house collection. Take your time when chamfering the trims as it may take several passes to get them just right.

Materials & equipment:

- Standard equipment and supplies (see pages 9 and 15)
- Translucent (2 blocks), Caramel, Terracotta, Gold, scrap or new clay, White and Black polymer clay blocks
- Cardboard to fit over tumbler or vase
- Tumbler or vase (at least 20½cm/8in high and 5cm/2in in diameter)
- Matte glaze
- Tweezers
- Acetate sheet measuring 2 x 12cm (¾ x 4¾in)

A note on the wood grain pieces

All the wood grain pieces should be baked at 100°C/212°F/Gas ⅛. After baking a veneered or chamfered trim, sand lightly to smooth the sides and to sharpen the corners. Always use extra-strong glue when directions call for glue.

1 To make wood grain, blend half a block of translucent with one quarter block of caramel; form into a log. Roll thin snakes of one-eighth block of terracotta cut to the same length as the log and place them along the log, spaced evenly around. With one-sixteenth block of gold, make snakes and position as before. Fold and roll this assembly several times to make wood grain. Roll a 3mm (⅛in) layer at least 18cm (7in) long. Mix further batches as needed to make the clock. (The grain should run along the clock length.)

2 Cut a piece for the base measuring 25 x 28 x 22mm (1 x 1⅛ x ⅞in) from scrap or new clay. With wood grain, veneer all around the 25mm (1in) sides; bake for 20 minutes.

3 Place a 6mm (¼in) high strip of wood around the bottom edge of the clock base; smooth the joins and square up the corners. Use a dowel or knitting needle to chamfer the top edge towards the clock base (see the main photograph

opposite as a guide for shaping). Trim the top edge, then press the edge of the blade into the base of the chamfered curve to make a sharp line all around the trim. Bake for 10 minutes.

4 Cut one piece measuring 3 x 14 x 18mm (⅛ x ⅝ x ¾in) for the case base and one piece measuring 18 x 14 x 18mm (¾ x ⅝ x ¾in) for the case top from scrap or new clay. Veneer one 14 x 18mm (⅝ x 3/4in) side on both pieces so that the clock base is 6mm (¼in) high and the clock top is 22mm (⅞in) high. Bake for 10 minutes.

5 Place the wood grain on the baking surface and cut three pieces measuring 18mm x 15cm (¾ x 6in) for the back and side panels. (For best accuracy, avoid moving the pieces before baking.) Bake for 10 minutes.

6 Glue one x 18mm (¾in) side of the case base (see Step 4) to one end of the back panel so that the veneered end of the case base faces towards the back panel and the edges are flush. On the other end of the back panel, glue the case top (see Step 4) so that the veneered end faces towards the back panel and the edges are flush. Leave to set, then glue the side panels onto the sides of the back panel, case top and base, and leave to set.

7 △ Cut a 25 x 30mm (1 x 1¼in) notch in the cardboard. The clock base should fit into the notch and the trim around the bottom base should keep the piece from falling through the notch. If possible, when you bake the clock, hang it upside-down from the cardboard and place the clock carefully inside the tumbler or vase with the cardboard resting on the rim. This will keep the long panels from bending and distorting during or after baking. If your oven isn't large enough, bake the clock flat or standing and then hang it from the cardboard to cool.

8 Glue the case base to the centre top of the clock base and leave to set. Wrap a 3mm (⅛in) snake of scrap or new clay around the case base where it joins the clock base. Cut one or more 12mm (½in) high strips of wood grain. Then, placing one cut edge about 6mm (¼in) below the top edge of the clock base, wrap the strips around the base, smoothing joins and sharpening the corners.

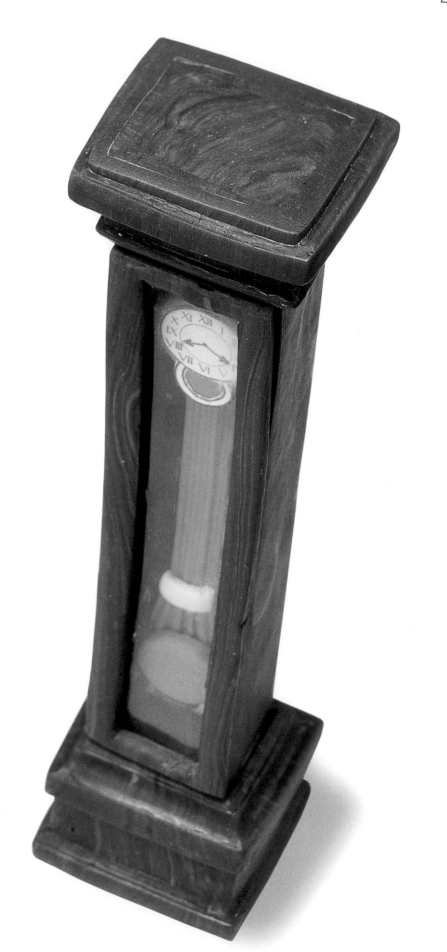

▶

11 Cut 6mm (¼in) high strips of wood grain and wrap them around the top of the case top, flush with its top edge. Smooth the joins and sharpen the corners. Hang (see Step 7) and bake for ten minutes. Cut 6mm (¼in) high strips of wood grain and wrap these around the strip that you have just baked, with the top edge about 3mm (⅛in) below the top edge of the case top. Chamfer the lower cut edge to curve it down towards the case top. Hang and bake for ten minutes. Then paint the inside and outside of the clock with matte glaze.

9 Beginning about halfway up the 15mm (⅝in) strip, use a dowel or knitting needle to roll and curve the wood grain up to the top edge of the base of the case all around the clock. Trim all round to make the wood grain the same height as the case base. Then roll carefully down from the top to make a uniform shallow curve around the top of the trim. Make a thin line at the bottom of the shallow curve with the blade as for Step 3. Trim the bottom edge evenly all round. Hang (see Step 7) and bake for ten minutes.

10 Cut 18mm (¾in) high strips of wood grain and, with the edges flush, veneer the case top. Hang (see Step 7) and bake for 10 minutes. Next, cut 4.5mm (³⁄₁₆in) high strips of wood grain and wrap these around the bottom edge of the case top. Chamfer the edges upwards and out towards the case top. Then roll from the top down to make a shallow curve at the top of the trim. Hang as previously described and bake for ten minutes.

12 Cut templates (see page 15) for the clock face, pendulum and pendulum weight from a 3mm (⅛in) layer of gold. Make a 1.5mm (1/16in) snake of gold, wrap this around the top circle of the clock face and flatten it slightly. Use a wool needle to press ridges in the pendulum, then round the cut edges of the pendulum to make it into a shallow dome. Cut the two curved templates from a 3mm (⅛in) layer of white and cut a rectangle measuring 3 x 9mm (⅛ x ⅜in) and a small, sharp triangle from 3mm (⅛in) layer of black. Centre the triangle against one long rectangle edge and press gently to join the pieces. Bake for ten minutes.

13 Glue the small clock face circle over the narrow cut edges of the pendulum and glue the small, curved white pendulum piece at the end of the narrow section. Then glue the weight over the wide cut pendulum edge. Finally, glue the black piece, point down, under the bottom edge of the pendulum weight and then glue the flat-bottomed white piece inside the clock case at the back bottom edge.

14 Make two x 9mm (⅜in) diameter balls of scrap or new clay. Press one at the back of the clock face and the other at the back of the pendulum weight. Then turn the clock face up and flatten the clay balls by pressing them against the baking surface. Turn the clock face down again and bake for ten minutes. When cool, remove the flattened balls and glue them back in place. Photocopy and cut out the clock face and glue it to the clay clock face.

Clockwise from top left: *case top, the completed clock and detail of base.*

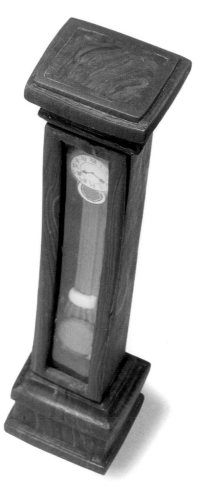

15 Spread glue on the flattened backs of the clay balls. Then, holding the narrow part of the pendulum with tweezers, lower the clock face and pendulum assembly into the clock case; position it and press into place.

16 Cut the door template from a 3mm (⅛in) wood grain layer. Smooth and round the inside cut edges, then bake for ten minutes. Paint with matte glaze and glue trimmed acetate to the back of the door piece for glass. Finally, glue the door to the front of the clock.

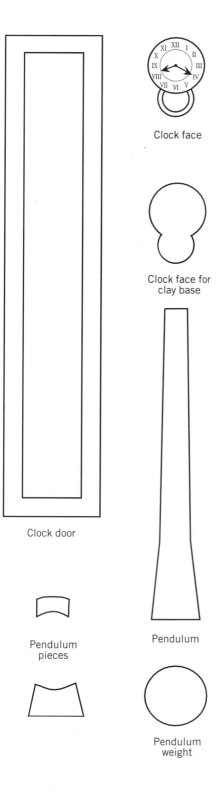

Clock door

Pendulum pieces

Clock face

Clock face for clay base

Pendulum

Pendulum weight

ribboned Christmas tree

Why not decorate your doll's house for Christmas? You could even design some beautifully wrapped polymer clay gifts to hide beneath it!

Materials & equipment:

- Standard equipment and supplies (see pages 9 and 15)
- Pine Green, Savannah, Brown, Carmine Glamour and White Glamour polymer clay blocks
- Adhesive tape
- Glitter
- Bowl with a small base, such as a rice bowl
- Potholders
- Wooden dowel or chopstick trimmed to 9cm (3½in) long
- Talcum powder
- 35mm (1⅜in) film canister
- Tweezers
- Gloss and matte glazes
- Rub-on gilding compound
- Leftover canes from other projects and several scraps of different polymer clay colours

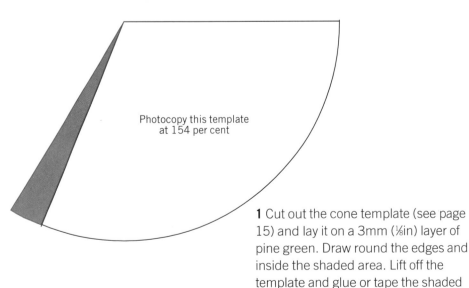

Photocopy this template at 154 per cent

1 Cut out the cone template (see page 15) and lay it on a 3mm (⅛in) layer of pine green. Draw round the edges and inside the shaded area. Lift off the template and glue or tape the shaded edge under the opposite edge to make a paper cone.

2 △ Next, cut out the pine green clay along the traced lines of the template. With a craft knife, cut 7mm (¼in) deep points in its curved edge. Wrap the clay around the paper cone with the cut points around the base and smooth the join. Use the edge of the knife to flick the cut points up and sprinkle them with glitter. Place the bowl upside-down, put the cone on top and bake for 10 minutes. Using potholders to protect your hands, pick up the bowl from inside the oven to avoid breakage, then leave to cool.

3 Remove the paper cone from inside the clay cone. Press a 2.5cm (1in) diameter ball of scrap or new clay inside the tree tip. Push the dowel or chopstick (for the tree trunk) into the soft clay so that the trunk is centred inside the cone and carefully remove the trunk.

4 From a 3mm (⅛in) layer of pine green, cut 12mm (½in) wide strips. Cut points in one long edge of each strip. Wrap strips around the cone, points down, with the straight edge about 6mm (¼in) higher than the previous round. Flick up the points; sprinkle with glitter. When two or three rounds are in place, put the cone onto the upturned bowl; bake for 10 minutes, then leave to cool. Repeat until the cone is covered with strips.

5 Glue the trunk into the impression made in Step 3. Sprinkle talcum powder inside the film canister. Press a 3.2cm (1¼in) diameter ball of savannah into the canister. Then press your finger into the clay and work it up the sides of the canister to form a pot with sides that measures no less than 3mm (⅛in) thick and about 2.5cm (1in) high. Shake the pot from the canister and bake for 10 minutes. When cool, sand the rim.

6 Place a ball of brown clay inside the pot. Press the trunk into the brown clay so that the tree is centred over the pot and its bottom edge covers the top of the pot. Carefully remove the trunk and bake the pot for 10 minutes. When cool, glue the tree trunk into the pot.

7 Roll about 40 balls of carmine glamour measuring 3–5mm (⅛–³⁄₁₆in) and bake for 10 minutes. When cool, pick up a ball with tweezers, place a dot of extra-strong glue on it and secure to the tree to resemble an ornament. Repeat until the tree is covered.

8 Place four small dots of white glamour evenly spaced around the tree, about 2.5cm (1in) from the bottom edge for markers. Cut 5mm (³⁄₁₆in) wide strips from a 1.5mm (¹⁄₁₆in) layer of white glamour. Then cut four 7.5cm (3in) lengths of these strips. Twist one piece gently and press the end of the strip over one of the markers and the other end over the next marker to form a swag. Repeat with the other three pieces so that the tree is surrounded with swags.

9 Next, cut four 2.5cm (1in) lengths of the strips created in Step 8. Cut notches in the ends and fold each one in half at an angle to resemble the ends of a bow. Press one of these at the peak of each swag.

10 Cut four 4cm (1½in) lengths of the strips created in Step 8. Fold the ends to the middle to resemble bows. Cover each middle with a short length of the strips from Step 8 to resemble knots and press the bows over the folded edges of the bow ends from Step 8. Cut eight 5cm (2in) strip lengths (see Step 8). Cut a notch in one end of four of the lengths. Press the unnotched end of one strip to the tree's tip so that the notched end drapes down the tree between two bows. Repeat for the other three notched lengths. Put the ends of one unnotched length together to form an open loop. Then press the ends to the tree top so that the loop drapes down the tree between the two notched strips. Repeat with the remaining lengths. Flatten a 6mm (¼in) diameter ball on the tip of the tree; bake for 10 minutes.

11 △ Paint the carmine ornaments with gloss glaze and paint the tree using matte glaze. Leave to dry. Apply rub-on gilding compound to the white bows and swags. Finally, make gifts using leftover canes and other clay scraps for a variety of box and bag shapes. Embellish the parcels with curls, bows, flowers and ribbons.

Victorian fireplace

Bring the charm and character of the Victorian era to your doll's house with this tiled fireplace and marble surround, complete with a little crack in the firewall. It's modelled on a real-life fireplace, even down to the soot marks.

Materials & equipment:

- Standard equipment and supplies (see pages 9 and 15)
- Translucent, Black, Granite, White, Pink, Champagne, Bordeaux, Ochre and Leaf Green polymer clay blocks
- Wadded paper
- Black and Ochre or Brown artist's pastels
- 15 x 12mm (½in) headpins
- Artist's paintbrush, size 0000
- Black acrylic paint
- Matte and gloss glazes

1 Make several batches of marble as follows: form one quarter block of translucent clay into a log. Roll a 3mm (⅛in) snake of black and cut four 1cm (⅜in) lengths. Roll one 5mm (³⁄₁₆in) snake each of granite and white; cut five 1cm (⅜in) lengths from this. Apply the cut pieces to the translucent log and roll to smooth. Twist the log until all the applied colours run almost perpendicular to the log, then fold the log in half. Roll, twist and fold five more times. Check the baking temperature of the translucent clay on the package and bake at that temperature throughout this project.

2 Roll out and lay a 2.5mm (¹⁄₁₀in) layer of black on a baking surface and cut out template A (see pages 15 and 37). Trim the sides at the dotted lines and replace them with marble strips. Lay the template on the top and trim again. For best accuracy, avoid moving the piece before baking. bake for 10 minutes.

3 Roll out and lay 3mm (⅛in) sheets of marble mixture on a baking surface and cut out rectangles following the grain of the marble roughly in the same direction as the first dimension given (see project photograph and Assembly Diagram A, page 36):
piece B – two 17.5 x 95mm (¹¹⁄₁₆ x 3¾in)
piece C – two 16 x 95mm (⅝ x 3¾in)
piece D – one 83 x 16mm (3¼ x ⅝in)
piece E – one 127 x 21mm (5 x 1³⁄₁₆in)
Piece E is the mantel. Chamfer its two

short edges and one long edge with a pencil or knitting needle so that the widest edge is at the baking surface. For best accuracy, avoid moving these pieces before baking and then bake for 10 minutes.

4 Cut a 2cm (¾in) square from a 3mm (⅛in) sheet of marble. Press and roll with a wool needle to achieve a cross section as shown next to template F (see page 37). Trim the edges, then cut two pattern piece F. Bake for 10 minutes.

5 Use extra-strong glue to assemble pieces A–F as shown in Assembly Diagram A.

6 From a 2.5cm (1in) block of scrap or new clay, cut templates G and H (see page 37). Bake for 10 minutes.

7 To construct the flower tile cane, roll a log 1.5 x 4cm (⅝ x 1½in) from pink. Wrap with a 1.5mm (¹⁄₁₆in) layer of champagne. Reduce to about 3mm (⅛in). Pinch the resulting snake between your fingertips to form a lens shape and cut into 5cm (2in) lengths.

a

b

5mm (³⁄₁₆in)

15mm (⅝in)

c

d

e

9 ▷ Roll a 3mm (⅛in) layer of champagne, 20cm (8in) long. Cut at an angle and position as indicated in the assembly diagram (see left). Wrap with a 1.5mm (¹⁄₁₆in) layer of champagne and wrap again with a layer of ochre. Reduce the cane to about 13mm (½in). Cut 10 5mm (³⁄₁₆in) slices. Make two lines of five tiles pressed together in a row. Bake for 10 minutes. Sand until very smooth and about 3mm (⅛in) thick. Reheat and remove from the oven. While the tiles are still warm, lay templates I over them and trim the angles. Glue the resulting pieces to G as shown (see page 37).

8 △ For the flower centre, from bordeaux, roll a log 5 x 15mm (³⁄₁₆ x ⅝in). Wrap with a 1.5mm (¹⁄₁₆in) layer of ochre. Reduce the resulting cane to 3mm (⅛in) in diameter and trim to 5cm (2in) long. Wrap the flower centre with the lens-shaped lengths to form petals (see above) until the flower is about 1.5cm (⅝in) in diameter. Roll a log 5mm x 20cm (³⁄₁₆ x 8in) from leaf green. Cut the log in half and insert a thin slice of champagne, then reassemble the log. Cut into 5cm (2in) lengths and place so that the flower has a leaf positioned at all four corners.

Top and above: *The completed fireplace in position.*

10 Cut one template J from a 3mm (⅛in) layer of black. Bake for 10 minutes. Glue G to the inside back of A as shown on page 37 so that the flower tiles angle inwards into the fireplace. Glue J in place on top of the two G templates. Lay a 3–5mm (⅛–³⁄₁₆in) snake of clay to fill the angle between the two Gs and J, and A. Cut a 5mm (³⁄₁₆in) wide strip of black and build a frame using A as the base and curving the frame up to the edges of G and J. Smooth into place. Use a ball stylus to make decorative indentations all around the frame. Bake for 10 minutes.

11 Cut two template K from a 3mm (⅛in) layer of black. With a long blade, mark several lines along the length of K. Put a snake of uncured clay on one edge of each K template and press them into place as shown on both sides of the fireplace (see page 37), where the uncured clay is shown as an oval.

12 Mix half a block of white with a pea-sized piece of ochre and a half-pea size piece of black. Roll a 3mm (⅛in) layer of this. Texture with wadded paper and cut out templates L and M. Brush with artist's pastels to suggest soot and cracks. Bake the L pieces only for 10 minutes. Glue the L pieces to the H pieces, then to the back of the fireplace as indicated (see Assembly Diagram B)

using uncured clay to aid placement. Cut N from a 3mm (⅛in) layer of black and place as the floor of the fireplace. Drape M over the back of the fireplace. Anchor the points of M, then bake the entire assembly for 10 minutes. If N falls off, glue back into place.

13 Cut O from black and mark dots with a headpin. Bake for 10 minutes. Turn O over and impress another layer of black to become template P. Glue O on top of N on the fireplace floor. Finish P's outline, poke the impressed holes with a headpin and bake for 10 minutes. Insert headpins into the holes. Lay a snake of black along O's row of dots. Press the headpins into the snake, positioning P as the top of the grille. Bake for 10 minutes, then paint the headpins black.

14 Cut templates Q and R from a 3mm (⅛in) layer of black. Lift the middle section of R to make a gentle curve. Prop the curve with a bit of rolled or wadded paper if necessary. Bake for 10 minutes. Spread glue on the side of Q marked on the template. With the narrow point up, glue the Q pieces as high up as you can on the K pieces. Glue R on top of the Qs as shown (see below). Paint the black sections of the fire surround with matte glaze and paint the flower tiles with gloss glaze.

Assembly diagram A

Assembly diagram B

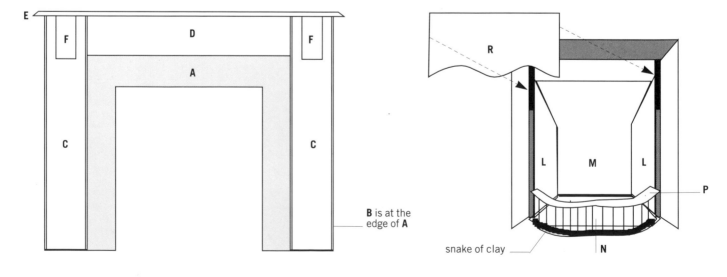

15 Cut a 7.5 x 10cm (3 x 4in) piece from a 3mm (⅛in) layer of black and cut tiles measuring 6 x 12mm (¼ x ½in) from a 3mm (⅛in) layer of leaf green. Lay three tile rows and position the fireplace behind the tiles. Impress into the black clay and remove the fireplace. Finish laying the green tiles and partial green tiles onto the outline. Bake for 20 minutes, then sand. Coat the tiles with gloss glaze, leave to dry and glue the fireplace into position.

How to assemble the tiles looking at template A from the top

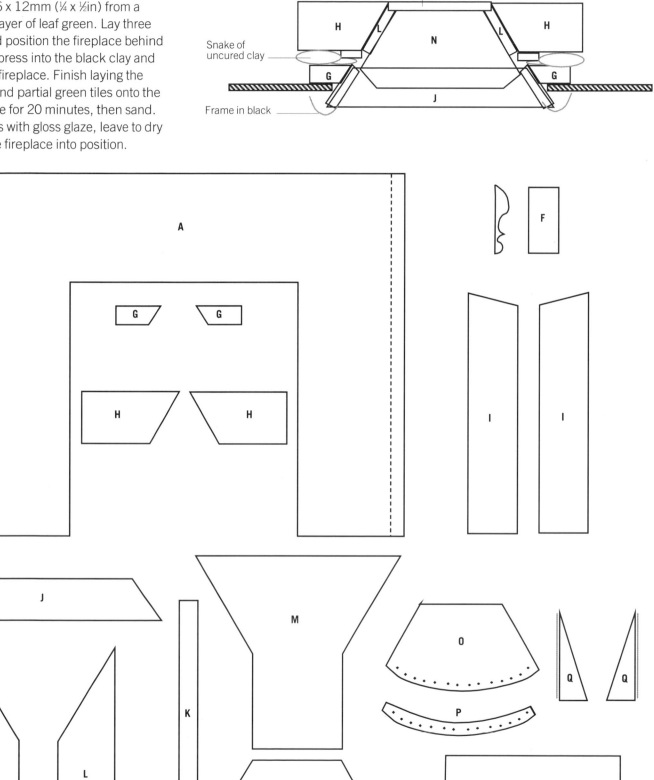

curious cat

This polymer clay cat, with its curious expression, is small enough to fit into any dolls' house. Incremental baking minimizes distortion as you work on this miniature cat. Try using a magnifying lamp when modelling tiny projects such as this.

Materials & equipment:

- Standard equipment and supplies (see pages 9 and 15)
- Gray or Silver polymer clay blocks
- Artist's paintbrush, size 0000
- Acrylic paints of your choice for eyes and fur
- Acrylic paints in black and pink
- Matte and gloss glazes

1 Roll a 6mm (¼in) diameter ball of gray or silver clay. To form the brow, roll a 2mm (⅛in) snake of clay and wrap it around the ball and trim. Place a short length of the snake on top of the ball to make the nose. Use the craft knife to smooth and blend the edges of the snakes into the ball. Press the nose down from the brow with the flat of the knife and push the end of the nose up to flatten it.

2 Next, roll three 2mm (⅛in) balls of clay and position them for the cheeks and chin. Smooth and blend the outside edges of the balls leaving the "Y" shape formed under the nose in place. Redefine the mouth, if necessary. Use the needle to make whisker dots on the cheeks and make eye indentations with the ball stylus. Bake for five minutes.

3 ▽ Make a neck by wrapping clay around the back of the brow and under the chin. Smooth and blend, shape the neck downwards and bake for five minutes. For the body, roll a clay ball about 20mm (¾in) in diameter. Flatten it to 7mm (¼in) thick. Trim one edge and flatten the base by standing the body up. Place the neck at the front of the body, and smooth and blend the edges.

4 Roll a 4mm (³⁄₁₆in) snake. Flatten and round one end and place in position for the shoulder. Carefully pull the snake to make the leg thinner. Lay the cat on its side and trim the leg 2mm (⅛in) longer than the leg. Use the blade to cut halfway through the leg, 2mm (⅛in) from the end. Push the end below the cut upwards to form the foot. Test the length by "sitting" the cat up and repeat for the other side.

5 Next, roll a 2mm (⅛in) snake, cut a 1.5cm (⅝in) length of clay and fold one quarter of the snake back on itself. Press onto the side of the cat's lower back to make a hind leg. Smooth the bent-back piece into the body. Roll and flatten a 6mm (¼in) ball of clay. Place this on the cat's hip against its hind leg and smooth and blend. Press the hip down and slightly over the leg. Repeat on the other side of the cat.

6 Roll a 2mm (⅛in) snake for the tail, cut a 32mm (1¼in) piece and taper one end. Press 6mm (¼in) of untapered end under the cat and smooth and blend. Smooth and blend the cat's back end over the tail on the upper side. Curve the tail as desired.

7 Cut small triangles measuring about 1.5mm (1/16in) thick and gently smooth the bases onto the back of the cat's head to make its ears. Use the ball stylus to carefully round the ear bases. Then use a craft knife to cut a tiny notch in the bottom of the outside of each of the cat's ears. Press the notch lightly together and then trim the tops of the ears, if necessary. Smooth the point at the top of each ear.

8 ◁ Make the toes by cutting three lines into the feet, then press them together lightly. Round the tips of the feet without making the toe lines disappear. Make sure the cat can still sit and that its front legs remain straight. Bake for 10 minutes.

9 Place a tiny drop of paint into the eye indentations. Leave to dry. Paint a black pupil in each eye and paint the nose and inside ears pink. With fur colour, outline the eyes and paint the rest of the cat with short strokes. Leave to dry, apply matte glaze over the fur, place a tiny drop of gloss glaze over the eyes and leave to dry.

3

jewellery

sea treasures brooches

The ocean is full of inspiration in the forms of fauna, flora and flotsam. Washed-up or washed-out pieces, such as this shard of willow-pattern china, need only a frame of polymer clay to become stunning brooches or pendants.

Materials & equipment:

- Standard equipment and supplies (see pages 9 and 15)
- Red Golden, Leaf Green, Green, Ivory, Hot Pink, Black and Gold polymer clay blocks
- Broken china
- Pin or brooch backs (available from craft stores)

1 To make the starfish brooch, form about half a block of red golden into a shallow dome, about 6.5cm (2½in) across. The dome should taper so that it is very shallow at the edges. Make the starfish template (see page 15) and lay it on top of the clay and cut it out. Smooth and round the arms of the starfish. Use the handle of a craft knife to indent the body between the arms. Trim and neaten the edges.

2 Place a 1.5mm (¹⁄₁₆in) diameter snake of leaf green along the centre of each arm, starting about 6mm (¼in) from the tip and stopping about 3mm (⅛in) from the centre.

3 Cut a 1.5mm (¹⁄₁₆in) diameter snake of green into 1.5mm (¹⁄₁₆in) long pieces and roll these into balls. Place five balls on the side of each green snake (see photographs). Flatten the balls with your fingertip. Roll two pieces into a ball and flatten the ball in the centre of the starfish's body.

4 Prepare the ivory pieces as the green pieces in Step 3. Place one ivory ball at the centre end of each green snake. Then place one ivory ball on the two pink dots at the end of each arm. Indent the centre of each ivory ball with the tip of a wool needle.

5 Place a 3mm (⅛in) diameter ball of black at the centre top of the starfish's body. Indent the centre of the black ball with the tip of a wool needle. Bake for 20 minutes and when cool, glue the pin or brooch back to the back of the starfish.

6 To make the china brooch, thoroughly wash a pretty, preferably flat china shard. Place it on a 3mm (⅛in) layer of gold clay. Working one side at a time until all sides are covered, wrap the clay up the side and over the top of the shard. Use the craft knife to cut a jagged trim in the gold clay (see photographs). Smooth the joins on the side. Wrap a 3mm (⅛in) snake of clay around the edges of the clay-covered shard, close to the top. Bake for 20 minutes. When cool, glue a pin or brooch back to the back.

Clockwise from top left: *Detail of starfish brooch, the two brooches displayed on a garment and close-up of the china brooch.*

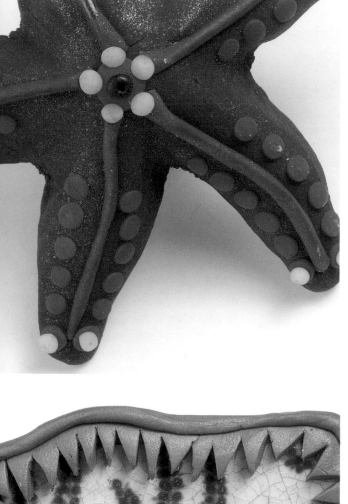

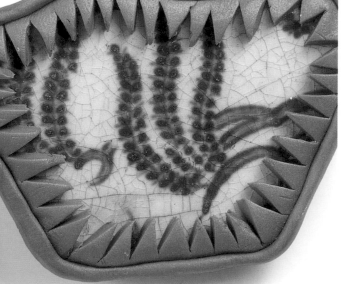

stony hair slide & earrings

Practical, as well as decorative, this faux-rhodochrosite hair slide looks particularly attractive in strawberry blonde hair. Copy this design or substitute blue, green or violet clays to suit other hair colours.

Materials & equipment:

- Standard equipment and supplies (see pages 9 and 15)
- Pink, Red, Golden Yellow, Yellow, Orange, Translucent (2 blocks), Mother-of-pearl and Terracotta polymer clay blocks
- Scrap clay, if desired
- 7.5cm (3in) long metal hairslide
- Drill with buffing wheel or gloss glaze
- Clip earrings with bases for gluing

General instructions

1 The term "pea-sized" in these directions refers to a piece that is one-eighth part of a sixteenth part of a 56g (2oz) block. Mix the following colours:
Mixture 1: One-sixteenth block of pink with a pea-sized piece of red
Mixture 2: One-sixteenth block of pink with a pea-sized piece of golden yellow
Mixture 3: One-sixteenth block of pink with a pea-sized piece of yellow
Mixture 4: One-sixteenth block of pink with a piece of orange the size of one-and-a-half peas.

2 Cut the mixtures into quarters, then cut a block of translucent into eighths and cut two of the eighths in half to make four-sixteenths. Mix one quarter of Mixture 1 with one-eighth block of translucent, then mix one quarter of Mixture 1 with one-sixteenth block of translucent. Now you have three versions of Mixture 1: the two remaining quarters (mix these back together), a medium-sized ball with some translucent clay and

a large ball with more translucent clay in it. Repeat with the remaining mixtures for 12 combinations.

3 Now make the following mixtures:
Mixture 5: One-eighth block of translucent with a pea-sized piece of mother-of-pearl, two crumbs of pink and one crumb of yellow
Mixture 6: One-eighth block of translucent with one-sixteenth block of mother-of-pearl, one quarter of a pea-sized piece each of orange and pink
Mixture 7: One-eighth block of translucent with two pea-sized pieces of mother-of-pearl
Mixture 8: cut the large ball of Mixture One in half and add half of a pea-sized piece of red
Mixture 9: translucent only.

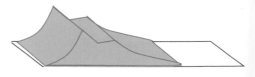

4 △ On a sheet of paper, mark a rectangle 7.5 x 2cm (3 x ¾in). With about half of Mixture 5, make a double-peaked shape within the rectangle (see above), with peaks off-centre and the base about 5cm (2in) long.

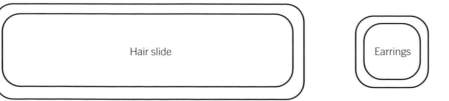

Hair slide   Earrings

5 From a 1.5mm (1/16in) layer of one of the colour mixtures above, cut a piece about 2cm (3/4in) wide and long enough to lay over the double-peaked shape from Step 4, plus a little on each side. With a wool needle, press ten or more grooves across the width of the piece.

6 With layers of varying thicknesses (13mm/1/16–1/8in), repeat Step 4 with different colour mixtures. Press each new layer into the grooves of the previous one using the wool needle. When the ends of the layers reach the borders of the marked rectangle, trim them so that the assembly builds upwards.

7 Roll a 3mm (1/8in) snake, 15cm (6in) long. Line up the snakes and cut a 7mm (1/4in) length of each. Bundle the pieces together to follow in the same direction, then stand the bundle on the last layer from Step 6, so that the snakes are perpendicular to the layers. Repeat until the vertical snakes cover the entire layer.

8 Add more layers to the assembly as in Step 6. If you wish to change the contours, fill some grooves with thin clay snakes in the same colour as the last layer. When laying the next piece of clay add a new contour in another place.

9 Roll 6mm (1/4in) diameter snakes of what remains of Mixture 7 and with one-sixteenth block of translucent. Wrap each snake with a thin layer of one of the colour mixtures, adding similar colours together, if needed. Reduce the wrapped snakes to diameters between 3mm (1/8in) and 4.5mm (3/16in). Cut them into 2cm (3/4in) pieces (or longer if your cane has widened). Lay the pieces across the width of the previous layer, following the contour of the piece.

10 Follow Step 8 using up the rest of the mixtures and the translucent clay. Mix similar colours together, if necessary, to make a layer. If you have a very deep contour, fill it in a little.

11 Tip the layered cane over on its side. Trim off the top at the base of the lowest contour to make a rectangular slab. Press and pull out the slab from its 2cm (3/4in) width to 4.5cm (1 3/4in) wide. Set the cane back upright and trim off one end to reveal the streaks underneath.

STONY HAIR SLIDE

1 To make the hair slide, mix one quarter block of terracotta with one eighth block of translucent and a pea-sized piece of pink. Make the hair slide template (see page 15) and, from a 3mm (1/8in) layer of this mixture, cut out the shape. Do not remove the template from the clay. Turn the piece so that the template is on the base and smooth the cut edges. Position the piece, still on the template, onto the hairslide. Bake for 10 minutes, then remove the paper template. When cool, sand the edges of the base.

2 From a 3mm (1/8in) slice of the cane from Step 11 (see general instructions), cut the shape inside the template. Centre the slice on the brown base. Press the top of the cut edges down almost to the base edge. Smooth the clay up and away from the edges to make a rounded effect. Bake for 10 minutes at 100°C/212°F/Gas Mark 1/8. Sand with increasingly finer grades of wet/dry sandpaper. Buff or seal with gloss glaze (buffing makes the clay more rock-like).

EARRINGS

For the earrings, follow the steps for the hair slide using the earring templates instead of the hair slide templates.

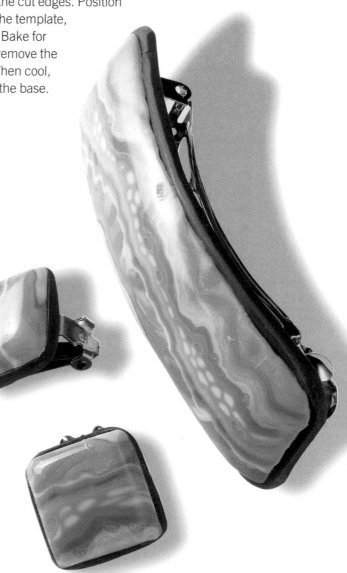

shiny earrings

Forget serviettes – now you can fold your earrings instead!
Add a little metal leaf beforehand (see Techniques, page 21)
for a truly elegant look.

Materials & equipment:
- Standard equipment and supplies (see pages 9 and 15)
- Light Green, Green Pearl and Turquoise polymer clay blocks
- Metal leaf in pink and gold swirl
- Small crystal beads, headpins, earring wires, jump rings, 8mm (⅓in) faux pearls, 6mm (¼in) gold-washed and croissant beads and clip earrings with bases for gluing
- Jeweller's round-nosed pliers and wire-cutters
- Matte or gloss glaze

General instructions

Each pair of earrings uses less than one eighth block of clay. Read the individual instructions and make the templates (see page 15) first. Roll a layer of clay to 1mm (⅟₁₆in) thickness, then apply metal leaf (see Techniques, page 21). If you add the metal leaf early on in the process, more clay will show between the metallic pieces. Then fold the piece in half so that the metal leaf is on both sides. Roll to a final thickness of 1.5mm (⅟₁₆in). Follow individual instructions for shaping. Where plain clay is used, it is the same colour as the metallized clay. All the earrings are baked for 20 minutes, then left to cool and sealed with matte or gloss glaze. For finishing, see below and for piercing before and after baking, see Techniques, page 18.

PINWHEEL EARRINGS

1 Using the template, cut two 2.5cm (1in) squares from the metallic layer. Make a diagonal slice at each corner. Fold one corner of each side (see open circles) to the centre (black circles). Press the corners in place. Press a 5mm (³⁄₁₆in) ball of plain clay into the centre with a ball stylus; pierce one corner.

2 To assemble, thread one crystal bead on a headpin. Trim the wire to about 7mm (¼in) from the top of the bead. Turn a loop in the wire. Open the loop of an earring wire by twisting it. From the loop, hang the crystal bead hanger and a jump ring. Open a second jump ring by twisting it and insert this into the pinwheel and the first jump ring, which is now hanging from the earring wire. Make sure the pinwheel will hang correctly, then close the jump ring.

PILLOW EARRINGS

1 Cut two 2.5cm (1in) squares from the metallic layer. Fold each corner (marked with an open circle) to the centre (marked as a black circle). Use a craft knife to press it into place. Press a 5mm (³⁄₁₆in) ball of plain clay into the centre with a ball stylus. Pierce one corner.

2 Thread one 8mm (⅓in) pearl bead on a headpin. Trim the wire to about 7mm (¼in) from the top of the bead and turn a loop in it. Open the loop by twisting it and from the loop, hang the pearl bead hanger and a jump ring. Open a second jump ring by twisting it. Insert the jump ring into the pillow and the first jump ring, which is now hanging from the earring wire. Make sure the pillow will hang correctly, then close the jump ring.

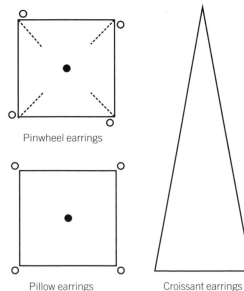

Pinwheel earrings

Pillow earrings

Croissant earrings

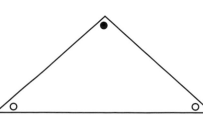

Two-fold earrings

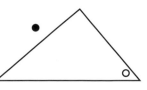

One-fold earrings

CROISSANT EARRINGS

1 Cut two triangles from the metallic layer using the Croissant Earring template. Roll each triangle from the base to the point, leaving a 5mm (³⁄₁₆in) hole (roll the triangle around a knitting needle for support, if necessary).

2 To assemble, thread a 6mm (³⁄₁₆in) gold-washed bead on a headpin with a croissant bead and another 6mm (³⁄₁₆in) gold-washed bead. Trim the wire to about 7mm (¼in) from the top of the last bead. Turn a loop in the wire and open the loop of an earring wire by twisting it. Hang the bead assembly from the loop and close it.

TWO-FOLD EARRINGS

1 Cut two triangles from the metallic layer using the Two-fold Earring template. Fold the corners at the base (marked with open circles) to the point (marked with a black circle) and press down gently. Then press a 5mm (³⁄₁₆in) ball of plain clay gently onto where the corners meet.

2 To assemble, glue the back of the piece to a clip earring base.

ONE-FOLD EARRINGS

1 Cut two triangles from the metallic layer using the One-fold Earrings template. Fold one base corner (marked with an open circle) over the opposite edge (marked with a black circle). Press a 5mm (³⁄₁₆in) ball of plain clay gently onto the other base corner.

2 To assemble, thread a 6mm (³⁄₁₆in) gold washed bead, a one-fold bead and a 4mm (³⁄₁₆in) gold washed bead on a headpin. Trim the wire to about 7mm (¼in) from the top of the last bead. Turn a loop in the wire. Open the loop of an earring wire by twisting it. Hang the bead assembly from the loop and close it.

Clockwise from top left: *Pillow, Pinwheel, One- and Two-fold, and Croissant earrings.*

tesserae bangles

Polymer clay artist Ester Anderson discovered the simple but effective technique of making tesserae using a clay gun to create these two textured bangles. I recommend that you use a soft clay, such as Sculpey III, for these projects.

Materials & equipment:

- Standard equipment and supplies (see pages 9 and 15)
- PVC pipe, 7.5cm (3in) in diameter, one piece 2.5cm (1in) wide and one piece 9mm (⅜in) wide (available from DIY stores)
- Leaf Green, Beige, Maroon, Terracotta and Ivory polymer clay blocks
- Clay extruding gun with square and triangular discs

WIDE BANGLE

1 Cover the inside of a 2.5cm (1in) wide piece of pipe with a 3mm (⅛in) layer of leaf green clay. Bake for 10 minutes.

2 Insert the disc with the square-shaped hole into the extruding gun. Make four different square-shaped snakes, cutting as needed to fit on the baking surface:
Square Shape 1: load one eighth block of beige into the clay gun, then one eighth of maroon for a maroon shape running through a beige outline
Square Shape 2: load one eighth of terracotta, then one eighth of beige
Square Shape 3: load one eighth of leaf green, then one eighth of maroon
Square Shape 4: load one eighth of terracotta and one eighth of leaf green.

3 △ Bake the square snakes for 5 minutes. While they are still warm, slice them into 1.5–3mm (¹⁄₁₆–⅛in) slices. Mix together all the little tesserae that you have just made.

4 Cover the outside of the PVC pipe with a 3mm (⅛in) layer of maroon. Press the tiles created in Step 3 into the soft maroon clay so that four tiles span the bangle width and the tiles are spaced fairly closely all around the bangle. Bake again for about 10 minutes.

5 Cover the cut edges with a strip of terracotta clay, rolled into a 3mm (⅛in) layer. Smooth the joins and seams. Bake for 15 minutes and sand, if desired.

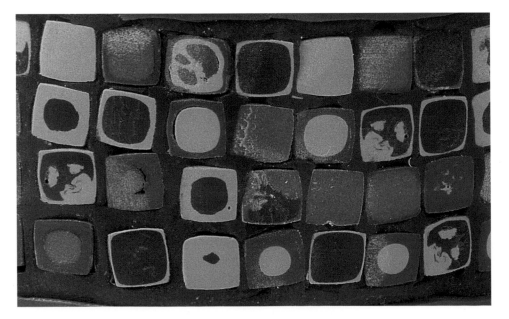

Left and opposite: *Close-up of one of the bangles and the finished bangles*

SMALL BANGLE

1 Line the narrow piece of pipe with ivory and bake for 10 minutes.

2 Insert the disc with the triangular-shaped hole into the extruding gun. Load one eighth block of maroon into the clay gun, then one eighth of beige for a snake with a beige shape running through a maroon outline.

3 Bake the triangular snake for 5 minutes. While it is still warm, cut it into 1.5–3mm (¹⁄₁₆–⅛in) slices.

4 Cover the outside of the narrow pipe with a 3mm (⅛in) layer of ivory. Press the tiles created in Step 3 into the soft ivory clay, placing the points of the triangles together to make little pinwheel squares which cover the entire outside surface of the bangle. Bake the assembly for 10 minutes.

5 Finally, cover the cut edges with a strip of maroon clay, rolled into a 3mm (⅛in) layer. Smooth the joins and seams. Bake for 15 minutes and sand, if desired.

VARIATION

Try some of the other clay gun discs for different designs or load more than two colours at a time into the clay gun. Use the tesserae technique to embellish containers, eggs, beads and other projects.

dark necklace

Glass and stone beads provide a bright contrast to the dark polymer clay squares in this understated necklace. Before you begin, read about millefiori in the Techniques section first (see page 22).

Materials & equipment:

- Standard equipment and supplies (see pages 9 and 15)
- Mother-of-pearl, Anthracite, Navy Blue, Ochre, Bronze, Gray, Terracotta and Black polymer clay blocks
- Nylon beading string and beading needle, size 11 hematite-coloured seed beads, oystershell end tips, 4mm (³⁄₁₆in) round hematite beads and necklace clasp
- Clear nail polish (optional)

General instructions

1 Roll a mother-of-pearl log about 15mm (⅔in) in diameter and 5cm (2in) long. Wrap with a 3mm (⅛in) anthracite layer.

2 Reduce the log to about 25cm (10in) long. Cut into four equal lengths, then stack the lengths together and roll. Repeat this step two more times, ending with a circular cane of about 6¼cm (2½in) long. Trim the distorted ends.

3 Wrap the cane from Step 2 with a 3mm (⅛in) layer of navy blue.

4 From 3mm (⅛in) layers of ochre and bronze, cut strips about 3mm (⅛in) wide and as long as the cane. Use your blade to lift the strips and lay them along the cane length, alternating colours.

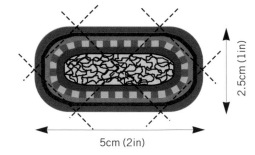

5 △ Wrap the cane from Step 4 with a 2mm (½in) layer of gray. Then wrap with a 1.5mm (⅙in) layer of anthracite. Finally, wrap with a 3mm (⅛in) layer of terracotta and trim the ends.

6 △ With the cane on its side, flatten it to an oval shape of about 2.5 x 5cm (1 x 2in). Stand the cane up on one end. Mark lines on the top (follow the dotted lines in the overhead diagram above). Cut down through the cane, first along the central "X" and then along the outside lines, taking care to keep your blade moving straight up and down as much as possible.

7 △ Wrap the resulting square canes with a 3mm (⅛in) bronze layer and then a 1.5mm (1⁄16in) layer of black. Reduce to 9mm (⅜in) square and cut into 7mm (¼in) slices. Pierce (see Techniques, page 18) and bake for 20 minutes.

Dark necklace

1 To make the necklace, use double nylon beading string. Cut a 1.25m (4ft) length of beading string, thread it on the needle and knot the ends. Thread one seed beed and tie it thoroughly at the end of the string. Take the needle through an oystershell end tip so that the bead rests inside the open halves of the end tip. Thread seed beads for 9cm (3½in). Repeat the instructions in brackets below until the necklace is about 10cm (4in) short of the desired length: (thread a 4mm/3⁄16in round hematite bead, a polymer clay bead from Step 7, another 4mm/3⁄16in round hematite bead and 3cm/1⅛in of seed beads). End with a 4mm/3⁄16in hematite round bead, a polymer clay bead, another 4mm/3⁄16in hematite round bead and 9cm/3½in of seed beads. Take the needle into another oystershell end tip so that the halves open away from the necklace. Thread a seed bead, nestle it into the oystershell and tie thoroughly.

2 Make a second necklace strand, going through the original beads in the oystershell bead tips and offsetting the hematite-polymer clay-hematite trios so that, as the necklace hangs, they fall between the ones on the first strand.

3 Dab extra-strong glue or clear nail polish on the knots and leave to dry. Trim the string and close the oystershells. Attach bead tips to the necklace clasp.

Above and below: *The dark necklace displayed on an evening bag and in detail.*

beads, beads

Beads come in so many shapes, sizes and colours that these only represent the tiniest fraction of what you can make. Let these examples inspire you and use the notes that follow to give you ideas for making beads from scratch or using leftover canes, tools and more.

General notes

• Millefiori cane beads (see page 22) should be thick enough for piercing. A good thickness is 6mm (¼in).
• To make barrel-shaped beads, insert a wool needle into a ball of clay. Holding the needle, roll the clay back and forth over your work surface until the sides flatten. Flatten the top and bottom, and roll again with the needle.
• For bicone-shaped beads, place a ball of clay on your work surface and use the smooth lid of a jar to roll the ball round and round. You may wish to drill the bead after baking to preserve its shape better (see Techniques, page 18).
• Finished beads should be baked for 20 minutes. Beads may be pierced before baking with a wool needle or after baking with a hobby drill. The following instructions will not refer to piercing and baking unless these procedures are different for individual beads.

Dark beads

Prepare and trim a cane as for Dark Necklace (see pages 50–1). Place the triangular cuttings back to back so that a black stripe runs from corner to corner on the bead. Wrap the new cane with ochre, then black or your chosen colour. Reduce, if desired, and slice.

Wrap the square trimmings (see Dark Necklace). Reduce the cane to about 9mm (¼in) square. Cut small slices and place them onto a ball of scrap clay.

Ladybird beads

Make a cane and black dots as for the Ladybird Light Switch (see pages 92–3). Reduce the cane to the desired size, slice the beads and add black dots.

Natasha beads

These square, mirror-image beads are named after the woman who popularized the technique used to make them. Use cuttings from any clay project and roll them into a log at least 12mm (½in) in diameter. Twist the log a few times and roll to smooth. Cut bead-length pieces and, for each piece, cut in half lengthwise. Cut the halves in half lengthwise and open out the halves so that the cut edges next to the curved surfaces are together. You will see the mirror image form on both sides of the joined cut. Put the two inside-out halves together so that the remaining sides also show a mirror image. The piece is now completely inside-out. Press the sides to fuse the bead.

South seas beads

For these, use leftover canes from the South Seas Cruet Set (see pages 78–9). Cover a scrap clay ball with slices of checked cane and roll to smooth. Then cover a scrap clay ball with slices of striped cane and roll into a barrel shape. Cut the striped cane into 6mm (¼in) slices and pierce one end. Then, with cane end trimmings, make Natasha beads (see above).

Stony bead

Dark beads

Snail bead

Natasha beads

Twirls

Red, white & blue twist beads

Make a candy cane twist (see page 20). Apply it to a white bead. Roll between your palms to smooth.

Twirls

Cut clay strips, wind around dowels, pierce and bake. When cool, loosen one corner and twist off the dowel. These beads were made with a pasta machine.

Stony beads

Prepare a cane (see pages 44–5). Wrap a 1.5mm (⅟₁₆in) slice around a ball of scrap clay and smooth the join. Gently pinch the slice together to cover the scrap clay. Pierce and roll into a barrel shape. If desired, add flattened balls of brown clay over the holes and repierce.

SNAIL BEADS

Condition one or more colours (pale colours look natural and stone effect colours are good too). Twist together gently, fold and roll until the piece has a fine striped grain. End by rolling a snake of about 10mm (⅜in) in diameter.

Cut the snake into 2.5cm (1in) pieces. Taper one end of a piece so that you end up with a cone-shaped piece, about 6.5cm (2½in) long, 10mm (⅜in) in diameter on one end and with a point at the other (see figure below).

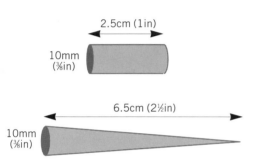

Hold a headpin at 45° against the large end of the cone with the head in the same direction as the cone's point. Wind the cone around the headpin so that the coils are close to each other like the coils of a shell (as though you are twisting the clay backwards). The first turn is hardest, but once you get it done, the rest of the cone will wind easily around the pin. Keep the shell as short as you can; don't worry about where the coil ends up on the headpin. Use your little finger to make a dip in the wide end of the shell. Bake with the headpin in place. After baking, remove the headpin with pliers and string the bead or trim the headpin and turn a loop in its end.

STAR BEADS

Cut small stars from a 3mm (⅛in) layer of clay using a blade or sugarcraft or ceramic craft cutters. If you want the stars to retain their sharp edges, bake them for 5 minutes. Apply the cooled shapes to a ball of uncured clay and roll to smooth. If you prefer more rounded edges, do not prebake before application.

GOLDEN ANTLER BEADS

Prepare a Skinner blend using brown, gold and translucent (see below and Techniques, page 21). After blending and rolling out, make a Swiss roll shape, beginning with brown and roll to smooth. With a wool needle, press and score deep lines around the outside of the cane to resemble the natural dips and lines on antlers. Bake for 5 minutes. While the cane is still warm, cut it into 6mm (¼in) slices. After piercing and baking, sand the cut surfaces.

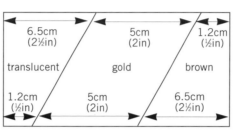

6.5cm (2½in) translucent	5cm (2in) gold	1.2cm (½in) brown
1.2cm (½in)	5cm (2in)	6.5cm (2½in)

METALLIZED BEADS

Apply metal leaf to a clay layer (see Techniques, page 21). Cut the clay into pieces and roll them into balls or barrels.

PURPLE, YELLOW & SILVER BEADS

Make a cane in the same way as Tiled Night-light Holders (see pages 62–3). Reduce to 6mm (¼in) square and cover a ball of scrap clay with thin cane slices.

MOKUME GANE (pinks & burgundy) BEADS

First, read the section on mokume gane in Techniques (page 20). Cover a ball of scrap clay with the first trimmings of a mokume gane assembly featuring layers of translucent clay tinted with shades of pink, burgundy and magenta separated by sheets of gold-coloured metal leaf.

Star bead | Purple, yellow and silver bead | millefiori bead | star bead | tesserae bead | mokume gane bead

South seas beads

Metallized beads

Mokume gane beads | South Seas beads | Dark round beads

Natasha beads | Red, white and blue twist beads | South seas barrel beads | Metallized barrel bead | Stony bead

Golden antler beads

Ladybird beads

buttoned up

Like beads, buttons are small packets of colour and design that beg to be collected and enjoyed. Polymer clay buttons cannot be dry-cleaned, so remove them before cleaning.

General notes

- Round buttons are made by flattening a ball of clay or cutting circles from a layer of clay. Use your thumb to flatten small balls. For larger buttons or for a more uniform look, use a smooth jar lid to flatten balls. Lightly dust the lid with talcum powder for easy removal.
- Experiment to find which size of clay ball flattens to the size of button you want. Remember that adding slices to a ball increases its size and the covered ball should be rolled to smooth it.
- Other shapes of button can be moulded, modelled or cut with a blade or shaped cutter.
- A thread channel is a dip in the middle of a button which makes it look a lot more button-like. To make one, indent the middle of your button with a marble, the end of a paperclip or the flat, round end of a writing pen or dowel. Pierce the thread holes within the outline of the thread channel. (I prefer buttons that are at least 3mm/⅛in thick for strength and so that the button is not left too thin in the middle after making the channel.)
- Pierce buttons with a wool needle before baking or drill after baking (see Techniques, page 18). If you are using a wool needle, pierce first from the top using a stirring motion, then pierce from the bottom.
- Bake the buttons for at least 30 minutes, then quench (see page 16). The instructions that follow will not refer to flattening clay balls, adding a thread channel, piercing and baking unless these procedures are different for individual buttons.

TURQUOISE & SILVER CUT-OUT BUTTONS

Roll a 3mm (⅛in) layer of stone-effect turquoise. With a clay cutter, cut out star shapes at 2.5cm (1in) intervals. Roll a 3mm (⅛in) layer of silver and place this under the turquoise layer. With a round cutter that is slightly larger than the star cutter, cut through both clay layers around each star. Use a ball stylus to make dots in the centre of each section between star points.

MOKUME GANE BUTTONS

Prepare a mokume gane assembly with layers of translucent clay tinted with earth tone clays separated by sheets of gold-coloured metal leaf. Texture, slice and flatten (see Techniques, page 20). Back the flattened pieces with a layer of black and cut into squares.

PATCHWORK BUTTONS

Make a patchwork cane as described in the millefiori section of Techniques (see page 22). Wrap the cane, then reduce, cut into quarters, stack into a new square cane and wrap the new square. Reduce to about 6mm (¼in) square. For a solid patchwork button, completely cover a scrap clay ball with thin cane slices. Otherwise, make a ball of clay with patchwork cane colours and place slices here and there on the ball of clay.

LEAF BUTTONS

Chop green, fluorescent green, leaf green and white clay into small chunks and press these together. Roll into a 3mm (⅛in) layer. Cut leaf shapes with a blade or leaf-shaped cutter and mark veins on the leaves using a wool needle.

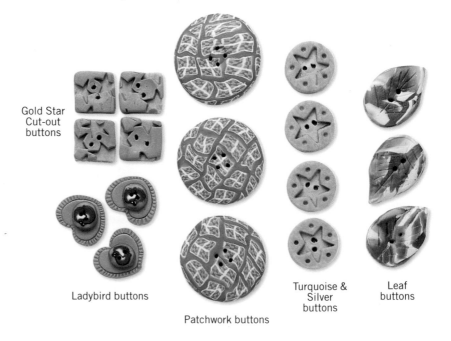

Gold Star Cut-out buttons

Ladybird buttons

Patchwork buttons

Turquoise & Silver buttons

Leaf buttons

"Tyre" buttons

South Seas buttons

South Seas buttons

Mokume Gane buttons

Button with Skinner Blend slices

Golden antler buttons

Red with black star button

Swirl buttons

Gold Star Cut-out buttons

Leaf buttons

Swirl buttons

Mokume Gane scrap button

Mokume Gane button

SOUTH SEAS BUTTONS

Prepare checked and striped canes as for South Seas Cruet Set (see pages 78–9). Pinch together the edges of the striped cane so that the black edges go all around it. Cover a ball of scrap clay with checked cane slices, then add slices of striped cane to divide the ball into quarters. Or make a ball of white or mother-of-pearl clay. Add striped cane slices but do not cover them completely.

LADYBIRD BUTTONS

From a 3mm (⅛in) layer of gold, cut heart shapes using a small heart-shaped cutter. Then use a smaller cutter to impress a line just inside the cut edge. With a wool needle, press grooves from the inside line to the outside edge to resemble a corrugated coin edge. Prepare a cane as for the Ladybird Light Switch (see pages 92–3) and reduce to 6mm (¼in) in diameter. Cut 3mm (⅛in) slices and press onto heart cut-outs. Pierce through the ladybird cane.

"TYRE" BUTTONS

Prepare a cane as for Dark Necklace (see pages 50–1). While it is still round, reduce to the desired button size, wrap with a 3mm (⅛in) layer of black and slice. Slightly smooth the cut edge. Use a ball stylus to make dots in the outer layer of the slice.

GOLD STAR CUT-OUT BUTTONS

Roll a 3mm (⅛in) layer of gold. With a small star-shaped cutter, punch out stars randomly but keep them quite closely spaced. Roll a 3mm (⅛in) layer of stone effect turquoise and place this under the gold layer. With a relatively large cutter of another shape, cut out buttons through both layers of clay.

SWIRL BUTTONS

Make separate snakes of two parts of a main colour and one part each of two or three contrasting colours. Stone effect shades, such as granite or lapis, are a good contrast because they add a little sparkle to the button. Put the snakes together and twist, fold and roll several times until you are almost satisfied with the striping. Make a snake about 9mm (⅜in) in diameter. Decide on your button size and cut cane slices 6mm (¼in) less than the finished button size. (For example, for a 15mm/⅝in in diameter button, cut a slice that is 9mm/⅜in long.)

Roll the slice into a ball and decide which side you like best. Place the ball on your work surface, best side up. Flatten it and if you do not like the look of the cut ends, pinch them closed before rolling the ball.

RED WITH BLACK STAR BUTTONS

Mix four parts translucent, three parts red, one part orange and a little black pepper. Roll into a ball and cover with black cut-out stars. Roll to smooth, flatten the ball and use the star cutter to make impressions on top of the button.

MOSAIC BUTTONS

Prepare square tiles as for Tesserae Bangles (see pages 48–9). Press the tiles into a 3mm (⅛in) layer of translucent and cut buttons around the tiles. Bake, leave to cool, then cover with a paper-thin layer of translucent, smoothing it over the edges and trimming. Bake again, then pierce with a drill.

GOLDEN ANTLER BUTTONS

Follow the instructions for Golden Antler Beads (see page 53), but pierce before baking. (Real antler buttons do not usually have a thread channel.)

Mosaic buttons

Swirl buttons

4

creative gifts

fantasy fish fridge magnets

With their twinkling eyes, these brightly coloured fish will use their magnetism to captivate you (and to hold all your papers firmly to the refrigerator). Glue a pin back in place of a magnet for a fishy brooch. Watch for images of fish in advertisements and books and use them to inspire designs for your own school of fantasy fish.

Materials & equipment:

- Standard equipment and supplies (see pages 9 and 15)
- Polymer clay in various colours (see individual fish instructions)
- Small magnets

General instructions

1 Build the fish up directly onto a tile or paper-covered tin and, as much as possible, use the craft knife instead of your fingers to place decorations. Make a 3mm (⅛in) layer of base colour, place the template on top and cut out the fish shape and a separate fin from this. Use your fingers to round edges and redefine sharp bends with the craft knife. Flatten the fins and tail slightly.

2 Make a 3mm (⅛in) layer of fish colour and cut out one or two fish shapes without fins and tail. Stack the layers of colour onto the base. Leave the fins and tail in the base colour, but smooth other colours to the edges and round the shape

with your fingers. With the point of the craft knife towards the fish's mouth, cut a wide U-shaped gill (see main photograph). Start about two-thirds of the way up the head and end almost at the bottom edge. Smooth the clay carefully under the gill.

3 ◁ Follow the instructions for each fish and refer to the photographs for eye, fin and decoration placement. Test eye sizes on the tile first. If the eye looks fine on the tile, roll the clay again and press it onto the fish. If not, adjust the amount of clay and try again. To make the reflection in the eyes, roll a tiny amount of white to a very small and sharp point. Lay the point on the eye, then use the craft knife to trim excess white away at the edge. Use a thin darning needle to make fin textures. With the needle point at the edge of the fish, press the needle into the fin and drag outwards. Trim jagged edges, if desired. Press the separate fin onto the fish and bake for 20 minutes. Finally, glue a magnet to the back of each fish and leave to dry.

CATFISH

- Tan (base), Ivory (fish colour), Red Golden, Blue Pearl, Hot Pink, Black and White polymer clay blocks

1 Cut the base from tan and two layers of fish colour in ivory using the template (see pages 15 and 61). (Do not cut gills on the catfish.)

2 Roll a 5mm (³⁄₁₆in) diameter snake of red golden. Slice thinly and place on top of the catfish's back (see photograph).

Roll a 2mm (¹⁄₁₆in) diameter snake of blue pearl. Slice thinly and place four blue pearl spots on top of each red golden spot (see photograph).

3 Next, make two 10 x 6mm (³⁄₈ x ¼in) oval-shaped irises of hot pink and place these on the fish's head. Make two black pupils and place these at the front edges of the irises and then add the reflections in both eyes with white.

4 Finally, use a darning needle to make two indentations at the front of the fish's snout. Roll two 2mm (¹⁄₁₆in) snakes of ivory, tapering them sharply at one end. Trim to 4cm (1½in) long, attach the blunt ends to the sides of the snout and rest the pieces upon the fins.

Below left: *Catfish;* below right: *The complete collection of fish.*

▶

STRIPED LADY FISH

- Hot Pink (base and fish colour), Leaf Green, Maroon, Ivory, Mint, Black and White polymer clay blocks

1 Use the template (see opposite) to cut a base and two top layers from hot pink without fins or tail. Roll hot pink into a ball and press this onto the fish's body to make a 1cm (⅜in) diameter spot.

2 Next, make 1mm (¹⁄₁₆in) snakes from leaf green, maroon and ivory. Taper the ends to a fine point. Place the stripes on the fish's body (see photograph) by first placing the point, then draping the snake to the edge of the body and trimming away the excess.

3 Make a 6mm (¼in) in diameter iris from mint and place this on the fish's head. Add a black pupil and a reflection in white. Make three eyelashes in the same way as the reflection and position as in the photograph. Repeat for the other eye.

4 Make two tiny balls from maroon and pinch them into a raindrop shape. Place them together to form the fish's lips, with a slight overbite. Use a craft knife to position the mouth on the fish and to push the pointed ends up into a smile.

5 Roll a 1mm (¹⁄₁₆in) snake of maroon and outline the fish's body from the front edge of the top fin, around the back and to the front edge of the bottom fin. Place the snakes about 2mm (¹⁄₁₆in) from the edge of the tail fins and the separate fin. Texture the fins by placing a darning needle on the maroon strip and dragging it out to the fin edges. Trim the tail and separate fin, then press the separate fin onto the fish's body.

BIG-EYE FISH

- Silver (base), Green Pearl (fish colour), Hot Pink, Blue Pearl, Tan, Black and White polymer clay blocks

1 Using the template (see opposite), make the base and one layer of fish colour from silver and green pearl. Smooth, then cut the gill.

2 Roll a 1mm (¹⁄₁₆in) snake of hot pink. Place this at eye level from just in front of the gill to the tail of the fish. Use the craft knife to smear and smooth the snake to make an indistinct streak on the body.

3 Next, roll a 1mm (¹⁄₁₆in) snake of blue pearl. Place cross hatches on the fish's body (see photograph).

4 Make a 1cm (⅜in) iris from tan and place this on the fish's face. Add a black pupil and white reflection.

5 Finally, make and attach a set of blue pearl lips to the fish. (To do this, refer to the previous instructions for the Striped Lady Fish.)

Catfish template

Striped Lady fish template

Big-eye fish template

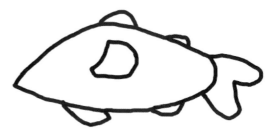

Scaled fish template

SCALED FISH

• Mint (base and fish colour), Pink, Green Pearl, Hot Pink, Black and White polymer clay blocks

1 Cut the base and one layer of the fish's head from mint using the template (see opposite). Smooth the head layer onto the base and taper the edge into the fish's body. Cut the gill and a smile (see main photograph). Trim the chin to about 2mm (1/16in) away from the snout.

2 Make 2mm (1/16in) layers of pink and green pearl. Trim these to about 2.5 x 3.8cm (1 x 1/2in). Stack green pearl on top of pink and cut a wedge off each short end. Make a Swiss roll shape (see Techniques, page 22) with hot pink on the outside. Reduce the Swiss roll to 8mm (5/16in) in diameter and trim the ends. Cut slices to use for scales. The Swiss roll will deform slightly as you cut it to make a perfect scale shape with a wide, flat edge and a rounded point on the other side.

3 With the rounded point towards the tail, place the first scale at the join of the fish's body and tail. The next row of scales should overlap the first so that none of the body colour appears between scales and should follow the same direction as the first. Allow excess clay to drape over the sides for now. Cover the rest of the fish's body as above with scales to end just short of the gill. Place a few more scales just above the gill to smoothly round towards the head and then trim.

4 Finally, make a 9mm (3/8in) iris from hot pink. Secure to the fish's head. Add a black pupil and reflection from white.

tiled night-light holders

In this project, translucent clay allows the candlelight to show directly through these tiled night-light holders, while metallic clay gives them a rich glow of their own.

Materials & equipment:
- Standard equipment and supplies (see pages 9 and 15)
- Translucent, Zinc Yellow, Purple and Silver polymer clay blocks

- Clear glass night-light holder or tumbler, at least 5.5–6cm (2⅛in–2⅜in) in diameter
- Garlic press (optional)

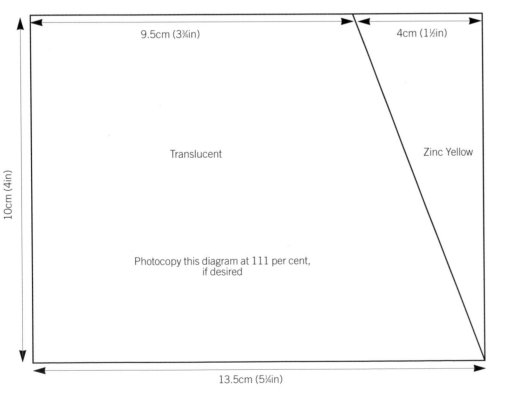

9.5cm (3¾in)

4cm (1½in)

10cm (4in)

Translucent

Zinc Yellow

Photocopy this diagram at 111 per cent, if desired

13.5cm (5¼in)

1 Make a Skinner blend as described in Techniques on page 21 with translucent and zinc yellow, placing the colours according to the diagram on this page.

2 Fold the blend accordion-style, starting with the yellow end about 2.5cm (1in) wide. Compress the folds and then mould the resulting cane into a triangle, about 2.5cm (1in) wide at the yellow base and 12mm (½in) high.

3 From a 3mm (⅛in) layer of purple, cut a strip measuring 1cm (⅜in) wide and as long as the triangular cane. Taper one long edge of purple. Split the translucent point of the triangle open at about 1cm (⅜in) and insert the tapered edge of the purple strip. Close the split point around the purple and then press back into the triangular shape.

4 Wrap the triangle with a thin layer (1.5mm/¹⁄₁₆in) of purple. Stretch and reduce the triangle to about 12cm (4¾in) long. Trim the ends, then divide into four equal lengths. Put the purple-strip points of these four triangles together to form a square with the yellow bases of the triangles on the outside of the square. Wrap the square cane with another thin layer of purple, then wrap it with a 3mm (¹⁄₈in) layer of silver.

5 Reduce the cane to about 17mm (⅝in) square. Place six cane slices evenly spaced around, about 7mm (⁵⁄₁₆in) below the rim of the glass night-light holder. Place two more rounds of six cane slices, centring them below the spaces between the previous round of slices.

6 Make 2mm (¹⁄₁₆in) rolls of silver by hand or by pressing the clay through a garlic press. Then make a lattice between the cane slices by placing the end of one roll at the bottom corner of a slice at the base of the glass, bringing it up diagonally across the three spaces and to the top corner of the cane in the top round of the glass. Place six such rolls in one direction, then place six more in the other direction.

7 Next, make a 3mm (¹⁄₈in) layer of silver, cut strips and place them around the top and bottom edges of the glass. Smooth the cut edges and joins and then bake for 20 minutes.

8 Finally, use any extra length of cane left over from this project to make another night-light holder or to decorate an egg (see pages 100–3).

VARIATION Substitute Fuchsia for Zinc Yellow, Sea Green for Purple and Gold for Silver. Cover the tumbler or night-light holder with slices of cane, leaving space at the top and bottom for gold strips. Omit the criss-cross strands, sand and buff.

sunset silhouette picture

You can follow the directions below to make this silhouette picture in exactly the same colourways or, alternatively, the lacy curtains and bowl of flowers would be just as charming if they were recreated in daytime colours with a shaded blue sky.

Materials & equipment:
- Standard equipment and supplies (see pages 9 and 15)
- Maroon, Carmine Glamour, Pink Glamour, Rose Glamour, White Glamour, Black, Black Glamour and Lilac Glamour polymer clay blocks
- Flower-shaped cutters, one small one (about 8mm/⅓in diagonally across) and one large one (about 18mm/¾in diagonally across)
- 12.5 x 18cm (5 x 7in) wooden photograph frame
- Spoon (optional)
- Olive gold rub-on gilding compound
- Soft cloth

1 Work this picture directly onto a baking surface or sheet of paper. Roll about 2.5 x 15cm x 3mm (1 x 6 x ⅛in) strips of maroon, carmine glamour, pink glamour, rose glamour and white glamour. Place the strips, one next to the other, in the order listed above. This sunset assembly is about 12.5 x 15cm (5 x 6in) wide.

2 Fold the sunset in half so that one end of each colour touches the other end (7.5cm/3in wide). Roll the folded strips out until they again measure about 15cm (6in) wide. Fold and roll out repeatedly until the lines between colours are indistinct. Place the template (see page 67) on the sunset assembly so that the maroon end is pointing upwards. Use a pencil to trace the outline of the window, the lines between window panes and the positions of the table, vase and flowers onto the clay. Remove the template and cut the window shape from the clay.

3 Next, cut strips from 3mm (⅛in) layers of black and position them over, under and to the left of the sunset window. Place the template over the clay again and mark the outline of the entire picture. Remove the template and trim the black clay. Mark vertical lines in the black clay using a long blade. Make evenly-spaced dots on the black to resemble a wallpaper design.

4 Roll 1mm (1/16in) snakes of black glamour. Place them over the traced cross-hatching on the window. If you have difficulty in rolling such small snakes evenly, roll them a little larger, then anchor them at one end of a cross-hatch and draw them out gently before laying them on the tracing. Trim the ends and then cut away from the table and vase outlines.

5 From a 3mm (⅛in) layer of black, cut a strip 4mm (3/16in) wide. Place this over the bottom border of the sunset window to cover the join and form the window sill. Cut away from the table leg.

6 Make the remaining items for the picture from black glamour. From a 3mm (⅛in) layer, cut strips 6mm (¼in) wide. Lay one strip for the table leg, the flange under the table and the table top. Then stack an additional strip on the table top.

7 Roll a 3cm (1¼in) ball. Slice off one third of the ball to form the body of the vase. Slicing will deform the rounded clay, flattening one edge and this is the vase top. Gently smooth the cut edge. Roll two x 8mm (⁵⁄₁₆in) balls and press them onto the bottom vase edge to form feet. Press the vase onto its outline on the picture so that the feet rest on the table top. Impress three flowers with the small flower cutter and make the centres with a ball stylus.

8 ◁ From a 1.5mm (¹⁄₁₆in) layer, cut a strip 2 x 25cm (¾ x 10in). Cut a lacy trim in one long edge using the larger flower cutter (see photograph). Then cut small flower shapes out of the centre of the strip. With the lacy edge pointing towards the sunset window, place one end at the end of the picture (see template, page 67) and the other end about 1.5cm (⅝in) short of the left side of the sunset window. Gather the clay between the two ends and then press it into place at the top of the curtain.

▶

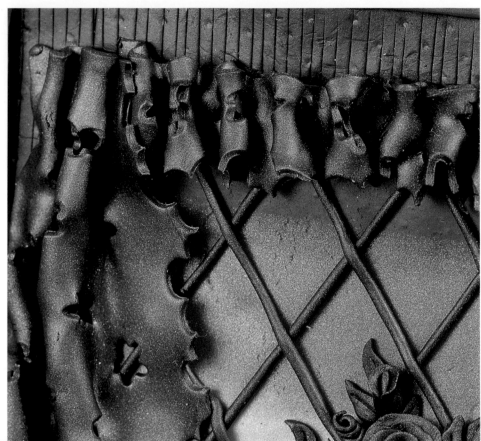

11 Cut 1mm (1⁄16in) slices from a 1mm (1⁄16in) snake. Position as on the template for small flowers (see opposite). Make a dent in the base of each floret with the craft knife. Roll three snakes, 1mm x 4cm (1⁄16 x 1½in). Twist each one around a wool needle to make a tendril. Gently push the tendril towards the needle point. Position as the template and press into place. Gently tease the twists apart and arrange them, referring to the detail photograph. Bake for 20 minutes.

12 Bake the wooden frame for 20 minutes at 130°C (250°F/Gas ½) to cure it. Cover it with a 1.5mm (1⁄16in) thick layer of lilac glamour taking care to press out any air trapped beneath the clay. Bake for 10 minutes. If bubbles appear in the clay after baking, use the back of a spoon to press them down while the piece is still warm. Sand if necessary. If the frame distorts, cracking the clay, fill the cracks with raw clay, sand and bake again for 10 minutes.

13 With 1.5mm (1⁄16in) layers of black, cover the outer side edge of the frame, folding the black onto the top, extending about halfway across the top surface of the frame. Use the cutters to make a lacy edge in the black all around the frame. Cut four small flower shapes and place them in the corners. Roll 1mm (1⁄16in) balls and press them into the flower centres. Bake for 10 minutes. With your fingertip, brush the black lace and flowers with rub-on gilding compound, then buff with a soft cloth.

9 Next, from a 1.5mm (1⁄16in) layer, cut a 6.5 x 15.5cm (2½ x 6⅛in) piece. Cut a lacy trim in the long edge on the right and the bottom edge. Then cut small flower shapes evenly spaced in the rest of the piece. Gather the top edge to fit as indicated on the template (see opposite) and arrange the folds and edges gently to resemble a drape.

10 Make the leaves, two rosebuds, three roses (make one with six petals and two with eight petals) and three spiky flowers in small, medium and large sizes (see Ruffles Name Plaque, pages 72–4). Roll a 6mm (¼in) ball to place under the spiky flower closest to the vase. Position the leaves and flowers as the template opposite and following the detail photograph on this page.

Above, below and opposite: *Close-up photographs showing the details of the drape, the flower arrangement and the edge of the frame*

14 Assemble the picture and frame, sanding the edges of the picture as needed to fit inside the frame. Use the frame's original backing if desired. If you remove the backing and prop the picture in a plate stand in front of a lamp, light will shine through the window to give a true sunset effect.

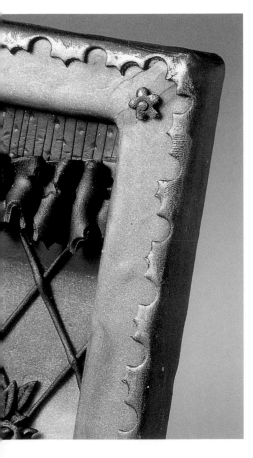

VARIATION

Use white shaded into blue for the window. Make the other picture items in daytime colours. Alternatively, use other cutter shapes to make different drapery designs.

Key to Sunset Silhouette Picture

 Rose

Rosebud

Leaf

 Spiky flower

Small flower

Tendril

clown cat trinket box

This dotted trinket box makes a practical and decorative gift. Before you begin to decorate the box with the clown cat, first paint it inside and out with red acrylic paint. Leave the paint to dry and then seal with acrylic spray glaze. Once the glaze has dried, cover the feet and line the inside of the box with a rich red felt.

Materials & equipment:

- Standard equipment and supplies (see pages 9 and 15)
- White, Black, Turquoise, Red, Lime, Hot Pink and Yellow polymer clay blocks
- Wooden box, about 11.5 x 6.5 x 8cm (4½ x 2⅝ x 3⅛in)

1 Roll a 3mm (⅛in) layer of white and use the templates (see page 15 and opposite) to cut out the cat's face and cheeks. Smooth the edges and roll two pea-sized balls of white.

2 Next, roll one 3mm (⅛in) layer each of black and turquoise. Cut irises from the turquoise and pupils from black. Add reflections to each eye (see page 58).

3 Press one white ball under each eye for padding, then place the cat's cheeks under the eyes and over the top of the padding. Smooth the cheeks into place. Use a darning needle to define the cat's smile and to make whisker holes. Then use your finger to indent the ears.

4 Roll two smaller than pea-sized balls of red. Press into place at the top outside corner of each cheek to make red cheeks (see opposite). Add the nose and bake the head for 20 minutes.

5 Make a 3mm (⅛in) layer of lime, about 30½cm (12in) long. Trim to 2.5cm (1in) wide and trim the ends straight. Roll small balls of all the other colours apart from lime. Press the balls thickly, but randomly onto the lime strip and flatten to make dots. Make separate dots by pressing at least 12 balls of each colour, apart from red, directly onto a baking tray or tile away from the lime strip.

6 △ Cut a piece of paper 2 x 2.5cm (¾ x 1in) and round the corners to make a collar template. Join the ends of the lime strip to make a ring (the seam will be at the back). Leave the back flat and gather up the rest of the strip evenly around the template (see photograph). Use a pencil to lift the edges to make ruffles. Roll a ball of lime as big as the end of your thumb and place it on the seam. Put the cat's head onto the collar, resting the ball of lime to test for placement. Remove the cat's head and bake the collar and dots of colour for 20 minutes.

7 Finally, glue the cat's head onto the collar and then glue the collar onto the box. Use the craft knife to slice the dots from the baking tray and glue these randomly onto the top and sides of the box.

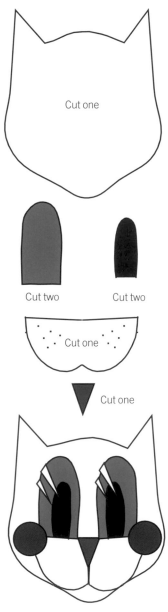

Cut one

Cut two   Cut two

Cut one

Cut one

Completed cat's face

Above and below: *Close-up showing the details of the cat's face and the completed trinket box.*

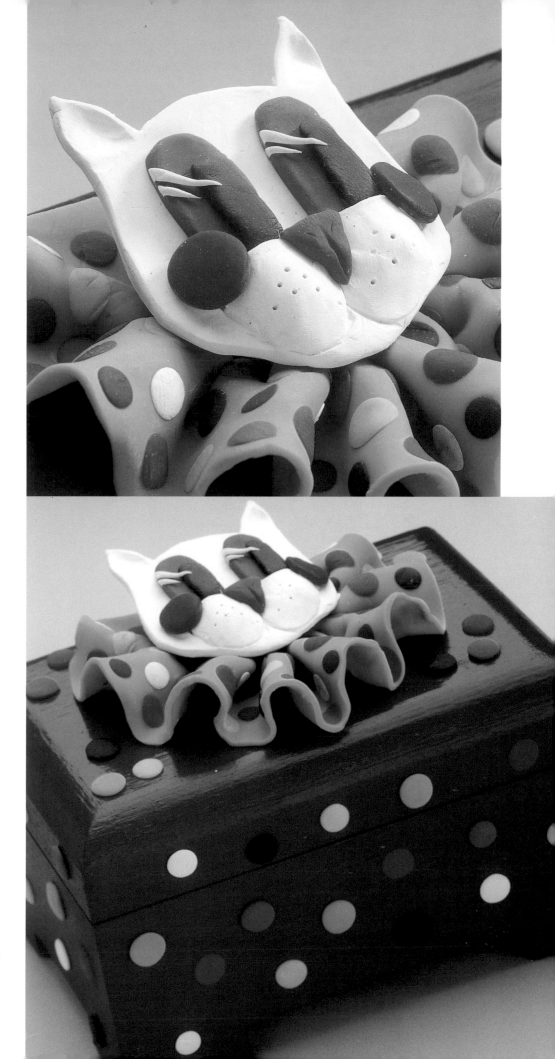

nautical flag box

This beautiful box would be perfect for storing jewellery collected from your travels. It was first painted inside and out with blue acrylic paint. White acrylic paint was sponged all over the outside and the box was then sealed with acrylic glaze. Once the glaze was dry, the box was lined inside with blue felt and this was also glued to the base.

Materials & equipment:

- Standard equipment and supplies (see pages 9 and 15)
- Red, Royal Blue, White, Golden Yellow, Translucent, Orange, Pink; plus optional colours: Terracotta, Silver and Caramel polymer clay blocks
- 28 x 9.7 x 7.7cm (11 x 3⅞ x 3in) long wooden box
- Various small seashells
- Scrap clay, for making moulds
- Toothbrush
- Adhesive tape
- Mother-of-pearl brush-on powder (optional)
- Artist's small paintbrush

1 Roll 3mm (⅛in) layers of red, royal blue, white and golden yellow. Cut them in the flag designs (see page 15 and opposite). Press the pieces together to secure. Bake for 20 minutes. Arrange on the box top to spell out the word "Trinkets" (see opposite); glue into place.

2 Make moulds from the seashells as described in Techniques, pages 20–1.

3 △ To make the ruffly coral, mix one quarter block of translucent with one eighth block of orange and one sixteenth of pink. Roll a 3mm (⅛in) layer roughly in the shape of a circle. Texture with a toothbrush. Make one cut from the centre of the circle straight out to the edge, then cut four wide petal shapes (see above).

4 △ Make offset columns of cuts in each petal. The outermost cut for every column goes through the edge of the petal. Then lift each petal into a ruffle with the craft knife, pulling gently to open the cuts into holes (see photograph). This piece should be no more than 7.5 x 10cm (3 x 4in). Prop the ruffles with cones of paper.

5 From the clay left over from the ruffle, add one sixteenth block of red and mix. Make another, smaller coral following the instructions above. Brush with mother-of-pearl powder, if desired.

6 Make a branch of coral by rolling a 6mm x 5cm (¼ x 2in) snake of red. About halfway up, cut away one third of the diameter to leave a stump. Bend the stump and the remaining branch away from each other. About 6mm (¼in) from the top, cut away half of the remaining diameter to leave another stump. Round the stumps as best you can and brush with mother-of-pearl powder, if desired.

7 Cast a few shell shapes (see Techniques, pages 20–1) using the following ideas or some of your own. The scallop is white marbled with a little of the coral mixture. For the pearly shell, use equal parts of silver and pink, then brush with mother-of-pearl before baking. The long shell is white, marbled with a little terracotta and brushed with mother-of-pearl powder before baking.

8 Finally, bake the coral and the shells for 20 minutes. Arrange them on top of the box first and then glue into place.

Above and below: *The completed trinket box and details of the shell shapes.*

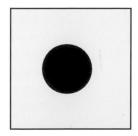

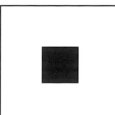

name plaques

You name it, and you can probably make it in polymer clay! Whether your preference is for ruffles and bows or sporting images, you can design a name plaque for a special friend. If you need inspiration for decorating a name plaque, sugarcrafting offers many design ideas that are easy to recreate in polymer clay.

Materials & equipment:

- Standard equipment and supplies (see pages 9 and 15)
- Polymer clay blocks in various colours (see individual plaques)
- Pinking shears or rotary cutter with pinking blade
- Picture wire, for hanging plaques
- Tracing wheel or stitching tool
- Gloss glaze

General instructions

For either of the following name plaques, trace the template (see pages 15 and 74) several times onto a sheet of paper. On the tracings, write the name that will appear on the plaque, centring it on the tracing. Choose the best version of your handwriting and cut it out as a template.

There are two ways to "write" a name in clay. The first way is to leave the template in place on the clay after trimming around it, then to use a pencil to trace the handwriting directly into the raw clay. Use the specified size of clay snake to "write" the name over the tracing. Press the writing very gently into the clay base so as not to flatten the snakes. The second way is to "write" the name with clay onto the paper, bake, then press the baked name into the raw clay base.

For letters with overlapping strokes, use a craft knife to push one stroke on top of the other (see the "a's" on the Ruffles plaque) or cut the clay after one stroke and reattach it when the line breaks free of the overlap (see the "n's" on the Ruffles plaque).

RUFFLES

- Rose, Pink, Lilac and Carmine Glamour polymer clay blocks, plus Light Green Glamour (optional)

1 First, roll a 3mm (⅛in) layer of rose glamour. Lay the oval template (see page 74) on top and cut around it. Mark the inner ring as a guide for the ruffle. Trace the name onto the clay unless you plan to bake the name separately.

2 Roll a 3mm (⅛in) layer of pink glamour. Cut two strips, 30.5 x 2.5cm (12 x 1in). Trim one long end of each strip with pinking shears or a pinking blade to make the strip about 2cm (¾in) wide. With the pinked edge out, gather and press the long straight edge of one strip halfway around the plaque on the marked line. Use a pencil tip to lift and arrange the ruffles in the pinked edge. Repeat with the other strip, folding its short ends under to disguise the joins.

3 With lilac glamour, roll 2mm (¹⁄₁₆in) snakes and "write" the name on the plaque or on paper. Roll a 3mm (⅛in) layer of carmine glamour. Cut a 6mm (¼in) wide strip; lay it over the gathered ruffle edge. Smooth away joins. Cut one piece 8.5 x 1.5cm (3¼ x ⅝in) and cut a V-shaped notch in each end. Fold into an upside-down V-shape and place the folded corner on the carmine trim.

4 From the same layer of carmine glamour, cut a piece about 2.5 x 7.5cm (1 x 3in). Gather the centre into a pleat and fold 13mm (½in) under on each end. Wrap a 1cm (⅜in) wide piece around the top of the pleated centre to look like the knot of a bow. Make sure the ends are hidden. Place the bow on top of the upside-down V-shape.

5 Next, make a decorative spray (see Steps 6, 7 and 8, and attach to the carmine trim if desired. (Use this to cover any awkward spots in the trim.) For the leaves, roll a 4mm (³⁄₁₆in) snake of light green glamour. Use the craft knife to make 1mm (¹⁄₁₆in) slices. Complete the leaves by pinching one end of each to a point. Use the craft knife to lift and position the leaves, then use the blade to press central veins. Make several leaves and then position them (see main photograph).

6 △ To make a rosebud, roll two x 5mm (³⁄₁₆in) balls of carmine glamour. Taper one 5mm (³⁄₁₆in) ball into a point to make a raindrop shape. Press the other one between your fingers to an oval shape thinning one edge to make a petal (see photograph). Hold the raindrop, point up. With the petal's thin edge at the same height as the raindrop point, wrap the petal around the raindrop, overlapping ends as necessary. Use your fingertip or a craft knife to flare the petal out and turn its edge down a little. Insert the tip of a darning needle into the side of the bud's base and use the darning needle to position the bud and press it into place.

Above and below: *The completed name plaques and detail photographs of the work.*

7 △ For the rose, make a rosebud as before from pink glamour. Roll five to eight more clay balls, 5–7mm (³⁄₁₆–⁵⁄₁₆in) in diameter. Flatten these into petals and wrap them around the rosebud, making one ring of three petals then another ring of two to four more petals offset from the first ring. Flare and turn the petals as before. Trim the base of the rose, insert the darning needle to position and press into place (see photograph). Make and wrap more petals for a larger rose.

8 △ To make a spiky flower, finger flatten a ball of lilac glamour to a strip about 1cm (³⁄₈in) wide and 2.5–3.5cm (1–1³⁄₈in) long (a longer strip makes a bigger flower). Trim one long edge to straighten it. Cut spikes in the other long edge and roll up the spiky strip (see photograph). Use the craft knife to flare spikes out in a flower shape. Position and press the flower into place by inserting a darning needle into its base.

9 Bake the plaque for 20 minutes. Make a hanger (see pages 19–20), bake this separately and glue to the back of the plaque.

Above and below: *Flower spray and hanger for the plaque.*

Ruffles name plaque base template

FOOTBALL NAME PLATE

- White, Black, Green, Yellow and Lime polymer clay blocks

1 Roll a 3mm (⅛in) layer each of white and black. Lay the football template on white and cut it out. Trace all the lines from the template onto the white clay with a pencil. Mark the black shapes with an "X". Remove the template and smooth the edges of the ball.

2 Lay the template on the black clay and trace around the black shapes. Use the craft knife first to cut around a marked shape on the white clay and lift it out, then use it to cut the corresponding shape from black clay and lay it into the white. Repeat until every marked shape on the white clay has been cut out and replaced by a black shape.

3 With the tracing wheel or stitching tool, carefully trace around each black shape and along the remaining traced lines on the white clay football to resemble stitching. Bake the football design for 20 minutes, then leave to cool. Paint the black shapes only with gloss glaze.

4 Next, roll a 3mm (⅛in) layer of green. Lay the base template onto the green, cut it out and trace the name onto the clay. Roll 3mm (⅛in) snakes of yellow and use these to "write" the name, placing them over the traced lines.

5 Roll a 3mm (⅛in) layer of lime. Cut a 5mm (¼in) strip and outline the green base. Smooth the joins. Roll 3mm (⅛in) snakes of lime and cut into about 20 pieces, from 3–8mm (⅛–⁵⁄₁₆in) long. Taper one end of each piece and place these dotted along the join between green and lime to resemble grass clumps. Use the craft knife to press a central vein into each grass blade.

6 Make four balls of green scrap clay about the size of your thumb end. Place on the green base in the area reserved for the football. Press them down with the white football until the ball rests about 6mm (¼in) above the base. Remove the ball; bake for 20 minutes. Glue the football to the four risers.

7 Finally, make a hanger (see Techniques, pages 19–20), bake the hanger separately and then glue it to the back of the plaque.

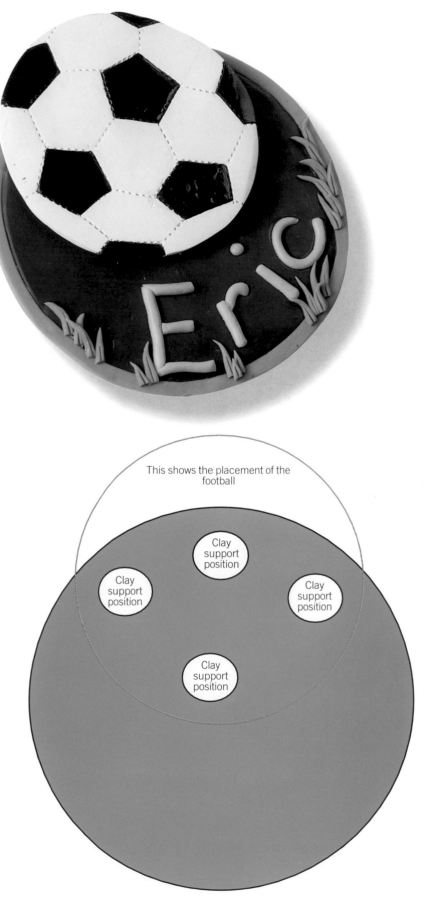

Football template

This shows the placement of the football

Clay support position

Clay support position

Clay support position

Clay support position

5

home accessories

south seas cruet set & napkin rings

Striped and checked canes give a pleasant impression of the motifs found on the islands of the South Seas. Vary the cane arrangement so that you can tell the difference between pots. In fact, why not make an entirely checked piece for the salt pot and a striped piece for pepper? The recipe given here should cover the salt and pepper pots and make at least four napkin rings.

Materials & equipment:
- Standard equipment and supplies (see pages 9 and 15)
- Orange, Red, Black (2 blocks), Champagne and Mother-of-pearl polymer clay blocks
- Glass salt and pepper pots
- Kitchen or bathroom paper roll cores

1 Mix up a rust colour from one quarter block of orange, one sixteenth block of red and a pea-sized piece of black.

2 To make the striped cane, from 3mm (⅛in) layers of black and champagne cut 12 strips, 7mm (¼in) wide and 5cm (2in) long. Stack the strips, mainly alternating colours but sometimes stacking two of the same colour together.

3 Next, turn the stack on its side and cover the side with 3mm (⅛in) thick sheet of black, a 3mm (⅛in) thick sheet of rust (mixed in Step 1) and a 3mm (⅛in) thick sheet of black. Turn the stack over and cover the other side with the same sequence of layers. Then trim the excess clay away all round.

4 For the checked cane, roll a champagne log, about 2.5cm (1in) in diameter and about 5cm (2in) long. Wrap the log with a 3mm (⅛in) layer of mother-of-pearl. Then wrap it with a 3mm (⅛in) layer of black.

5 Stretch and reduce the cane to measure about 20cm (8in) long. Cut into four equal lengths. Place two lengths side by side and stack the other two on top of those. Pinch and press into a square cane. Reduce, cut and stack as before to make a cane with 16 squares in its cross section.

6 Decide where you want to position the striped cane strips on the pots (see photograph as a guide). Cover the surface with checked cane slices, 3mm (⅛in) in size, reserving space for the striped cane. Insert the striped cane in the appropriate spaces, trimming away checked slices, as necessary. Press the slices together gently to cover any uncovered spaces. Bake for 20 minutes. Leave to cool, sand with increasingly finer grade sandpaper until smooth, then buff with a cotton cloth.

7 To make the napkin rings, cut a kitchen or bathroom paper roll core into 2.5cm (1in) slices. Line the inside with a 3mm (⅛in) layer of black. Bake for 10 minutes and leave to cool.

8 △ Cover the outside of the core with a 3mm (⅛in) layer of black. Then cover the surface of the uncured black clay with 1.5mm (¹⁄₁₆in) slices of checked cane. Trim, if necessary, and bake for 10 minutes.

9 △ From 3mm (⅛in) layers of black, cut 1cm (⅜in) strips. Cover the rims of the napkin ring with these strips, brushing the inside edge with your fingertips to smooth. Trim the outside edge, if necessary. Repeat to make four napkin rings, then bake for 10 minutes. Leave to cool, then sand and buff as before.

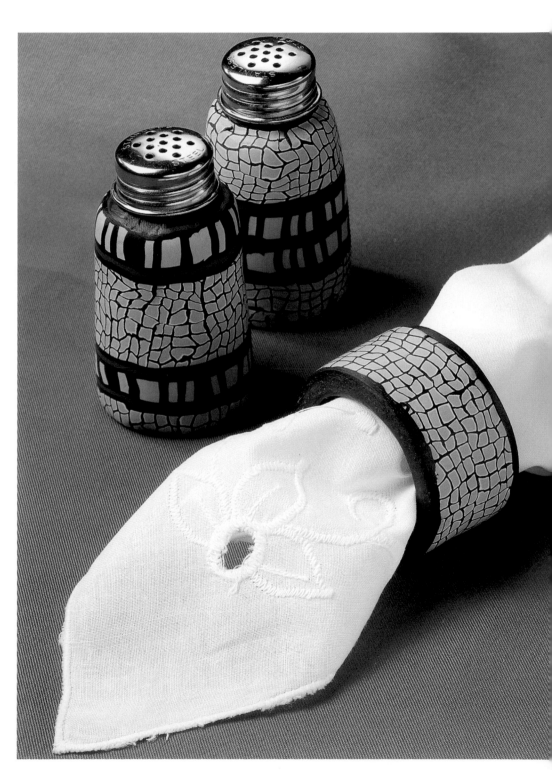

tiled cutlery

This cane recipe covers two or three knife, fork and spoon sets and there is enough to make a set of matching napkin rings (handwash only). For napkin ring directions, see page 79. If you wish to cover more sets, increase the width of the cane by about 4cm (1½in) per set.

Materials & equipment:

- Standard equipment and supplies (see pages 9 and 15)
- 3 or 4 matching knife, fork and spoon sets
- Scrap or new clay
- Mother-of-pearl, Blue, Light Blue, Golden Yellow and Orange polymer clay blocks
- Matte glaze

1 Cover the cutlery handles with a 3mm (⅛in) layer of scrap or new clay. Trim and smooth the surface, then bake for 10 minutes. Leave to cool, then sand to smooth again.

2 △ To make the cane, trim a 1mm (½₀in) layer of mother-of-pearl to 9 x 12cm (3½ x 4¾in) long.

3 Roll a 3mm (⅛in) snake of mother-of-pearl about 5cm (2in) long. Wrap this with a 1.5mm (¹⁄₁₆in) layer of blue and roll to smooth. Reduce the resulting wrapped snake to measure 1.5cm (¹⁄₁₆in) in diameter.

4 Make a 1mm (½₀in) layer each of blue, light blue, golden yellow and orange. These layers should be as wide as the mother-of-pearl layer in Step 2 and no more than 1cm (⅜in) long. Make another 1mm (½₀in) mother-of-pearl layer as wide as the layer in Step 2 and about 10cm (4in) long. Cut strips as needed for Step 5.

5 △ Turn the mother-of-pearl layer from Step 2 so that one 9cm (3½in) side is towards you for the bottom edge. Taper the edge by pressing it with your fingers. Beginning about 6mm (¼in) from the bottom edge, lay strips and snakes, one next to the other, towards the top edge as follows:

7mm (¼in) strip of mother-of-pearl
three 1.5mm (1/16in) strips of light blue alternating with the same width strips of mother-of-pearl
1cm (⅜in) strip of mother-of-pearl
5mm (3/16in) strip of golden yellow
5mm (3/16in) strip of mother-of-pearl
Two lengths of wrapped snake created in Step 3
1.5mm (1/16in) strip of mother-of-pearl, then another length of wrapped snake
1cm (⅜in) strip of mother-of-pearl
3mm (⅛in) strip of orange
3mm (⅛in) strip of mother-of-pearl
3mm (⅛in) strip of orange
11mm (7/16in) strip of mother-of-pearl
1cm (⅜in) strip of light blue
3mm (⅛in) strip of mother-of-pearl
3mm (⅛in) strip of golden yellow
3mm (⅛in) strip of mother-of-pearl
3mm (⅛in) strip of golden yellow
1cm (⅜in) strip of mother-of-pearl
5mm (3/16in) strip of blue

Roll up the layers from the bottom edge, smooth the join and wrap the resulting cane with a 1mm (1/20in) layer of orange.

6 Make a 3mm (⅛in) layer each of mother-of-pearl and light blue as wide as the cane and about 5cm (2in) long. Cut 3mm (⅛in) strips and lay them alternately all the way around and along the length of the cane. Then wrap the entire assembly with a 1mm (1/20in) layer of blue.

7 Reduce the cane made in Step 6 to 1cm (⅜in) in diameter, as needed. Cut 1.5cm (1/16in) slices and place these down the front of the length of the covered handle of each utensil, keeping the round shape of the slices as true as possible, with their edges touching each other. Cover the sides of the utensil, placing slices next to the joins of the original slices and fold them around the back of the utensils. Fill in remaining spaces as best you can. Press to fill any spaces left between slices.

8 Bake for 10 minutes. Leave to cool, then sand with successively finer grade sandpaper until the handles are very smooth. Seal with two coats of matte glaze, allowing the glaze to dry thoroughly between coats.

drapery finials

There's no need to spend a lot of money to achieve elegant drapery accessories. A little metal leaf and a few clay leaves will soon turn ordinary wooden finials into wonderful window ornaments.

Materials & equipment:

- Standard equipment and supplies (see pages 9 and 15)
- Ball-shaped wooden drapery rod finials, about 18cm (7in) in circumference
- Scrap or new clay
- Black or Green Pearl and Copper polymer clay blocks
- Pink and Gold Swirl metal leaf
- Dowel (optional)
- Matte or gloss glaze

1 Bake the finials in an oven preheated to 130°C/250°F/Gas Mark ½ to remove any moisture (this prevents the clay from bubbling up). Leave the finials to cool.

2 Make a 3mm (⅛in) layer of scrap or new clay, about 15cm (6in) square. Lay the template (see page 15) on the clay; cut it out. Drape the clay over the finial, press out trapped air, and press the cut edges together to cover the ball. Repeat for the other finial. Bake for 10 minutes. Leave to cool. Sand to smooth, if necessary.

3 Now make a 3mm (⅛in) layer of black or green pearl clay. Apply metal leaf to the top (see page 21). Roll the layer until it is about 1.5mm (⅟₁₆in) thick and 15cm (6in) square. (The metal leaf will crack.) Cut the finial template shape from this layer. Drape the metallized layer over the finial and gently press the cut edges together to avoid distorting the metal leaf.

4 From a 3mm (⅛in) black or copper layer, cut 12 leaves using the template. Starting at each leaf tip, drag a wool needle along the outside edges of the leaf and drag the needle at intervals into the leaf to form serrated edges. Mark a central vein on each leaf with the needle. Apply the leaves to each finial, with their bases at the base of the balls and their central veins over the seams of the metallized clay. Trim and bake for 20 minutes.

5 Then, from two 3mm (⅛in) black or copper layers cut two strips, 7.5cm (3in) long and 2.5cm (1in) wide. Wrap these around the slender neck between the finial base and the ball base at both ends. Trim and smooth the seams. With a pencil or dowel, press the clay against the neck of the finials.

6 Finally, from a 3mm (⅛in) layer of black or green pearl, cut two strips, 7.5cm (3in) long and 2cm (¾in) wide. Wrap them around each of the finial bases, and trim and smooth the seams. Bake for 20 minutes. Leave to cool, then seal the metallized portions with glaze.

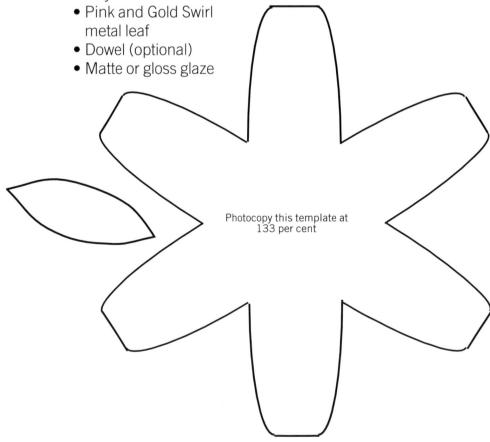

Photocopy this template at 133 per cent

rosy bathroom jar

A glass jar is hidden inside this rose-patterned clay sachet to hold powder, cotton balls or pins in your bathroom or bedroom. You could use home-made or commercial millefiori in place of roses. Reserve a 1cm (⅜in) wide slice of cane for the knob, then reduce the cane before slicing. Choose background and lid colours to match the cane.

Materials & equipment
- Standard equipment and supplies (see pages 9 and 15)
- Fuchsia, Fluorescent Red, Cadmium Yellow, Fluorescent Green and White polymer clay blocks
- Small glass jar
- Tape measure

1 △ To make the roses, roll a layer each of fuchsia and fluorescent red. Trim to 2.5 x 7.5cm (1 x 3in). Place the fuchsia layer onto the fluorescent red layer and taper the ends. Roll a 3 x 25mm (⅛ x 1in) snake of cadmium yellow and place it at one tapered end of the layers. Roll into a Swiss-roll shape, smoothing the ends so that the fluorescent red is all around the outside. Reduce to 7mm (¼in) and trim the ends. Roll a 3mm (⅛in) snake of fluorescent green and press along the side of the Swiss roll. Pinch to form a triangle and to make the rose cane.

2 Measure the jar from just below the rim, down the side and across the bottom, then up the opposite side to just below the rim. If the measurement is 15cm (6in) or less, one 56g (2oz) block of clay will be enough, whereas more than this means extra clay. Prepare a circular paper template using the measurement as the diameter. Fold the template in half, then in half twice more, to divide the circle into eighths. Roll a 3mm (⅛in) layer of white and place this on a piece of paper. Lay the circular template on the clay and cut out a circle. Mark the eighth-folds at the very edge of the clay. Place a sheet of paper over the clay circle and flip it over.

3 Gently press the bottom edge of a jar to mark the base of the container. Place slices of the rose cane on the white clay, leaving a clear 6mm (¼in) around the edges and the already-marked centre. Use the craft knife to press the flattened slices back into a round shape. Then use the point of the craft knife to make a vein in each leaf. Place a sheet of paper over the rose-covered clay and roll it gently to press roses into the white clay (do not flatten completely).

6 To make the lid, roll a 3mm (⅛in) layer of fluorescent red. Press the top of the covered jar into the layer to mark it. Cut out a fluorescent red circle just inside the mark, then roll a 3mm (⅛in) fuchsia layer and cut a circle about 1cm (⅜in) larger than the fluorescent red circle all round. Bake both circles for 20 minutes. Glue the fluorescent red circle to the centre base of the fuchsia circle.

7 Finally, make another Swiss roll as before but do not reduce this and do not add a green triangle. Trim to about 1cm (⅜in) wide. Roll two balls of fluorescent green of about 1cm (⅜in) in diameter, flatten and use your fingers to press to a point at one end. Use a needle to draw leaf veins in the green. Arrange the leaves and Swiss roll (see photograph below). Bake separately for 20 minutes and then glue to the centre of the lid.

4 △ With the paper still on top of the rose-covered clay, turn it over. Peel the paper off the bottom of the clay. Place the jar in the centre of the clay circle. Bring up the clay edge and press one edge mark against the jar below the threads for the lid (see photograph). Repeat on the opposite side of the jar, then repeat for the edge marks at 90° angles to the originals. Finally, repeat for the remaining edge marks so that you have eight points touching the jar and eight clay bulges. Press the bulges against the edge of the jar to form pleats and trim the top evenly.

5 Roll a 3mm (⅛in) layer of fuchsia. Trim to cover the pleat edges up to the rim of the jar and wrap around, smoothing the join. With a needle, make a hole in the clay at the base of the jar, then another towards the base of the pleated section and a third in the fuchsia collar. Bake for 20 minutes.

sun & sea wall clock

In this project, the ancient art of mosaic tiling is made simple with the use of a curved craft knife for cutting and laying the polymer clay tiles. Once the preparatory work is done, it's surprising how quickly you can lay the tiles. The technique was pioneered by polymer clay artist Sue Heaser.

Materials & equipment

- Standard equipment and supplies (see pages 9 and 15)
- Light Turquoise (2), White, Yellow, Golden Yellow, Ochre, Light Blue, Mother-of-pearl, Blue, Mint, Lilac, Violet, Black, Royal Blue, Dove Gray and Translucent (2) polymer clay blocks
- Clock movements (available from craft stores)
- Picture wire

General instructions

Trace and cut out the template on page 89. Roll a 3mm (⅛in) layer of light turquoise and place it on a tile. Lay the template on top and cut around the outer edge. Mark the centre, then cut a hole in it using the threaded bolt from the clock movements as a punching tool. Bake for 20 minutes and leave to cool. Using pea-sized chunks of clay, make the following colour mixtures: White/yellow, golden yellow/ochre, light blue/mother-of-pearl, blue/light blue, mint/light turquoise, light turquoise/lilac, lilac/violet and violet/a touch of black.

Roll 3mm (⅛in) layers of all the mixtures and small amounts each of mother-of-pearl, yellow, golden yellow, light blue, blue, royal blue, mint, light turquoise, lilac, violet and black.

1 Mix half a block of dove gray with one-and-a-half blocks of translucent. Roll a 3mm (⅛in) layer of the mixture. Place the rolled layer over the baked and cooled light turquoise layer. Trim and cut the centre hole. Lay the template over this layer and trace all the lines and rectangles.

2 Cut 12 rectangles roughly 7 x 17mm (⁵⁄₁₆ x ⅔in) of mother-of-pearl and place them on the rectangles marked around the edge of the clock. Use a straight edge to make sure opposite blocks line up with each other. Press a small dot of black onto the rectangle at 12 o'clock.

3 Next, read the general instructions for making polymer clay mosaics on page 23 of Techniques. For the waves, cut strips of the appropriate colour 4–5mm (³⁄₁₆–³⁄₁₆in) wide. To make the square tiles that make up the sun, cut strips measuring 1–2mm (¹⁄₁₆in) wide.

Clockwise from top left: *Mosaic sun, the completed clock and close-up of the work.*

4 Cover the top two wave outlines with mint. Add golden yellow reflections on the waves, where marked. Under the mint rows, place a row of mint/light turquoise mix, a row of alternating mint/light turquoise with light turquoise, then one or two rows of light turquoise. The lower wave shades further into light turquoise/lilac.

5 Cover the other two waves with lilac. Add golden yellow as marked. Under lilac, place a row of lilac/violet, a row of alternating lilac/violet and violet, and two rows of violet. Fill the remainder with the violet/black mix.

6 Fill the centre of the sun with a small circle of mother-of-pearl tiles (see photograph). The remaining rows of the sun and sky are worked around this circle as follows:
round 1 – yellow/mother-of-pearl
round 2 – yellow
round 3 – golden yellow
round 4 – golden yellow/ochre
rounds 5 and 7 – light blue/mother-of-pearl
rounds 6 and 8 – golden yellow
round 9 – alternate golden yellow with light blue/mother-of-pearl.

8 Work the remaining rows with the tiles turned perpendicular to the last row with the short end towards the sun: round 32 – repeat (five x blue, one x royal blue), rounds 33 and beyond – increase the number of royal blue tiles around the original with each row. Fit the blue tiles between the royal blue sections.

9 Roll a 3mm (⅛in) layer of black. Cut strips 5mm (³⁄₁₆in) wide and wrap them around the outside edge of the clock disc to hide the layers showing at the sides. Smooth joins. Cut some more strips and place them around the edge of the clock face with their outside edges at the outside of the black frame and their inside edges covering the edges of the mosaic. Smooth the joins and make decorative impressions around the strip with a ball stylus or some other texturing tool. Bake for 20 minutes and cool.

10 Determine the correct placement of the clock works and mark these on the back of the clock face (9 o'clock and 3 o'clock are in the sky just above the waves). Glue the clock works onto the back of the clock. Thread the bolt onto the spindle, then the hands and finally the spindle's cap. Make the hanger as wide as the clock movement (see Techniques, pages 19–20) and glue this to the back of the clock with two-part epoxy glue.

7 The tiles will now widen gradually until they are as long as the wave tiles and the rounds will be broken as they approach the waves and clock face edge. Continue working in rounds, curving the current round against the previous one:

rounds 10 and 11 – light blue/mother-
   of-pearl
round 12 – alternating light blue/mother-
   of-pearl and light blue
rounds 13, 14 and 15 – light blue
round 16 – repeating around (three x
   light blue tiles, one x light blue/blue tile)
round 17 – light blue only
round 18 – alternating light blue and
   light blue/blue
round 19 – light blue/blue only
round 20 – repeating around and offset
   round 16 – (four x light blue/blue,
   one x light blue)
rounds 21, 22 and 23 – light blue/blue
round 24 – repeating around – (three x
   light blue/blue, one x blue)
round 25 – light blue/blue only
round 26 – alternating light blue/blue
   and blue
round 27 – blue only
round 28 – repeating round and offset
   round 24 – (four x blue, one x light
   blue/blue)
rounds 29, 30, 31 – blue.

Opposite top and bottom: *Close-ups showing the placement of the mosaics; above and below: The clock in situ and diagram showing how the colours are arranged on the clock face.*

First solid round of light blue/blue mix

First solid round of light blue

First solid row of blue

Navy chevrons begin here

easy picture frames & candle-holder

Push-moulds come in all sorts of designs – flowers, fruit, butterflies and vegetables, to name but a few. With a push-mould, polymer clay and a little paint, you can customize some simple frames and make a matching candle-holder.

Materials & equipment:
- Standard equipment and supplies (see pages 9 and 15)
- Purchased push-moulds for polymer clay, one with berries and one with decorative hearts (available from craft stores)
- Talcum powder
- Glass candle-holder
- Red, Leaf Green, White and Rose Quartz polymer clay blocks
- Leaf Green and Yellow acrylic paints
- Artist's paintbrush, size 0000
- Matte and gloss glazes

- Clip frames (we used 20.5 x 44cm/ 8 x 10in and 12.5 x 18cm/5 x 7in with 10 x 15cm/4 x 6in photographs)
- Matte board or coloured paper, trimmed to fit inside the frames as picture mounts
- Pearlescent brushing powder

1 First, read the section on moulding polymer clay (see Techniques, pages 20–1) then dust the moulds with talcum powder before you begin to press the clay inside. For the strawberry frame and candle-holder (quantities for these given in brackets), mould and trim seven (three) large strawberries and four small strawberries from red, 15 (six) large leaves and nine small leaves from leaf green, and three (two) large flowers and three small flowers from white. Bake for 20 minutes, then leave to cool. Sand the bases, if necessary, to smooth.

2 Paint two coats of leaf green acrylic paint onto the leafy strawberry tops. Brush leaf green paint lightly onto the leaves to highlight the texture. Paint seeds on the strawberries and the flower centres using yellow acrylic paint.

3 Coat the leaves, flowers and leafy strawberry tops with matte glaze and leave to dry. Brush gloss glaze onto the strawberries, then brush gloss glaze onto one half of each leaf and dot each flower petal. Leave to dry.

4 Clean the glass in the frame thoroughly. Mark the position of the photograph on a piece of scrap paper cut to fit the glass. Place it underneath the glass and arrange berries, leaves and flowers onto the glass to fit around the photograph space. Use the photograph opposite as a guide or arrange as you like. Glue the pieces to the frame with two-part epoxy. Leave to set. Finally, assemble the frame with the picture and matte board or coloured paper.

5 △ Clean the candle-holder well, then arrange berries, leaves and flowers carefully around the base. Glue with two-part epoxy and leave to set according to the directions provided.

6 ◁ For the heart frame, mould and trim five large hearts using rose quartz stone effect clay. To preserve the scalloped trim around the hearts, press the flat of the craft knife point between scallops, then trim away the excess with the knife angled to cut slightly under the edge. Brush pearlescent powder on the borders and centre heart decoration. Bake for 20 minutes, then leave to cool. Sand the heart bases, if necessary, to smooth them.

7 Coat the hearts with gloss glaze, leave to dry and then arrange them in a row on the cleaned glass as in the photograph above or as desired. Use two-part epoxy to secure the hearts to the glass and leave to set. Finally, assemble the frame with the photograph and place matte board or coloured paper behind it as a display mount.

ladybird light switch

This colourful light switch cover would make a cheerful addition to a child's room. You could also make the design up into a stencil for other accessories in the room or create your own beads and buttons (see pages 52 and 54).

Materials & equipment:

- Standard equipment and supplies (see pages 9 and 15)
- Small electrical screwdriver
- Light switch cover
- Green, Mother-of-pearl, Fluorescent Red, Red, Bordeaux, Black, White and Fluorescent Green polymer clay blocks

1 First, remove the switch if it is attached to the switch cover. With a 3mm (⅛in) layer of green, cover the light switch cover and press out any trapped air. Trim the edges and trim away from the switch opening; bake for 20 minutes. When cool, sand until smooth.

2 △ Trim and arrange 3mm (⅛in) layers of mother-of-pearl, fluorescent red and red (see Figure 1). Blend using the Skinner technique (see page 21). Starting with the mother-of-pearl end, roll the clay strip until you reach the fluorescent red section. Begin wrapping clay only part-way around the roll every now and then (see above). This causes the mother-of-pearl to be off-centre, which will create a shine on the ladybird's shell. Wrap the roll with an extra red layer made from one quarter block of red.

3 Trim and arrange 3mm (⅛in) layers of red and and bordeaux (see Figure 2). Blend using the Skinner technique. Beginning with the red end of the clay strip, wrap the roll from Step 2, continuing partial rounds every now and then. Press, roll to remove trapped air and trim the ends.

4 Stand the roll on its end, position the mother-of-pearl 'shine' as if it were at about 4 o'clock. Hold the blade ends between the fingertips of both hands parallel to you and cut the roll in half.

5 Place a 1.5mm (¹⁄₁₆in) black layer to cover one cut edge of the roll for a line between the ladybird's wing cases. Trim, then make a 1.5mm (¹⁄₁₆in) black snake; pinch into a triangle. With the mother-of-pearl 'shine' still at 4 o'clock, lay the triangle along the edge at 9 o'clock. Put the roll halves together to form a cane, pressing to remove trapped air.

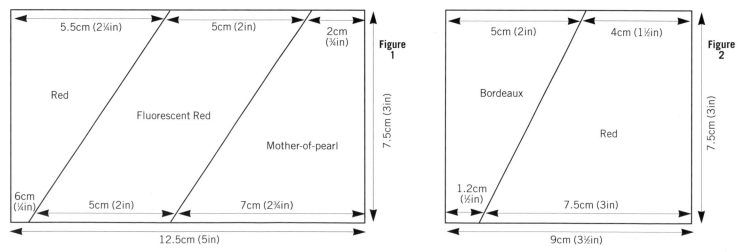

Figure 1

5.5cm (2¼in) | 5cm (2in) | 2cm (¾in)

Red

Fluorescent Red

Mother-of-pearl

7.5cm (3in)

6cm (¼in) | 5cm (2in) | 7cm (2¾in)

12.5cm (5in)

Figure 2

5cm (2in) | 4cm (1½in)

Bordeaux

Red

7.5cm (3in)

1.2cm (½in) | 7.5cm (3in)

9cm (3½in)

6 Wrap the cane from Step 5 with a 3mm (⅛in) black layer. From 3mm (⅛in) layers of black, cut a 6mm (¼in) wide strip as long as the cane. Centre this over the central black layer opposite the black triangle and along the cane length.

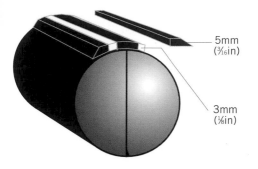

5mm (³⁄₁₆in)

3mm (⅛in)

7 △ From a 3mm (⅛in) white layer, cut two 3mm (⅛in) wide strips as long as the cane. Place on either side of the black strip in Step 6. From 3mm (⅛in) black layers, cut two 5mm (³⁄₁₆in) wide strips. Holding your blade lengthwise and at an angle along the top of each strip, cut a wedge off one side of the strip. Place trimmed strips along the outside edges of the white strips, trimmed side out, as shown in the diagram above.

8 Next, from a 3mm (⅛in) black layer, cut a 12mm (½in) strip. Trim away the corners along both sides of the strip, then lay it along the cane to cover the 6mm (¼in) black strip and the two mother-of-pearl strips. Cover the ladybird head with a 1.5mm (¹⁄₁₆in) black layer and smooth joins with your fingers.

9 From 6mm (¼in) diameter fluorescent green snakes, pinch wide triangles and lay these along the sides of the head to fill the space and to make the cane roughly oval-shaped. Wrap the resulting cane with a 3mm (⅛in) fluorescent green layer. Then wrap the cane again with a 1.5mm (¹⁄₁₆in) green layer. Roll gently to smooth but do not make the cane round again.

10 If necessary, reduce the cane to about 4cm (1½in) at the widest point and trim the ends. Cut one slice to about 3mm (⅛in) wide. Reduce to the dimensions shown in the table (see below) and then cut exactly the number of slices indicated.

Cane Diameter	No. of Slices
22mm (⅞in)	1
14mm (⅝in)	2
12mm (½in)	3–4
10mm (⅜in)	6–8
6mm (¼in)	10–12
5mm (³⁄₁₆in)	14–18

11 Arrange the slices from the largest to the smallest (see photographs). Make a black snake, 3mm (⅛in) in diameter and bake for 5 minutes. While it is still warm, cut into 3mm (⅛in) slices. Press the slices into the ladybird slices to form dots (see photographs). Bake the assembled light switch for 20 minutes and leave to cool before reassembling.

crazy quilt mirror

Make several polymer clay "fabrics" following the designs on these pages or create some to match your own decor. Piece them together to create a crazy quilt to frame a mirror or picture for a clever way to avoid sewing!

Materials & equipment

- Standard equipment and supplies (see pages 9 and 15)
- Copper, Pearl, Blue Pearl, Burnt Sienna, Beige, Ecru, Raw Sienna, White, Green Pearl, Cadmium Red, Black, Ultramarine Blue and Gold polymer clay blocks
- Print roller
- Mirror measuring 20 x 20cm (8 x 8in)
- Plate stand

1 Place small balls of white on the copper square at roughly 20mm (¾in) intervals. Flatten to 9mm (⅜in) diameter spots (experiment on your work surface first to achieve the correct size before placing the spots on the clay); offset the next row and repeat until the copper is covered. Flatten a green pearl ball to form spots of about 7mm (⁵⁄₁₆in) in diameter on the same edge of each white spot.

2 Make a candy cane twist with green pearl and cadmium red (see page 20). Reduce to no more than 1mm (¹⁄₁₆in) in diameter. Break when necessary. Arrange the resulting twists onto the pearl square in a squiggly pattern.

3 Roll a 3mm (⅛in) copper snake. Place a thin slice on the ecru square. Repeat until the ecru is densely covered.

General instructions

With one quarter block each of copper, pearl, blue pearl, burnt sienna, beige, ecru and raw sienna, roll a roughly square 3mm (⅛in) thick layer. Place the squares on pieces of copier paper to make them easier to move around. Then prepare seven "fabrics" according to the directions on these pages. Place a sheet of paper over each one in turn and flatten slightly with the print roller.

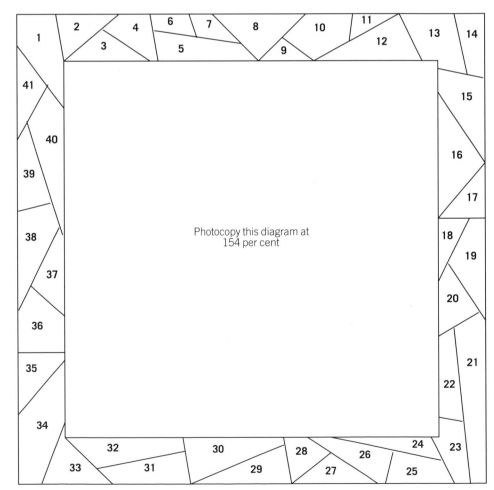

Photocopy this diagram at 154 per cent

10 To make the inside border, roll a 3mm (⅛in) layer of gold. Cut 12mm (½in) wide strips to fit inside the frame. Push the strips against the frame. Cut the points with the craft knife and remove the trimmed clay.

11 For the outside border, roll a 3mm (⅛in) layer of gold. Cut 25mm (1in) strips to fit outside the frame. Push the strips against the frame. Wrap them over the edge of the mirror and underneath it. Mitre the corners and trim the back of the mirror to straighten the edges.

12 To complete both borders, cut 4mm (³⁄₁₆in) wide strips of gold. Lay the strips over the "seam" between the frame and the points on the inside border and over the "seam" between the frame and the edge at the outside border. Mitre the corners and slightly flatten a ball of gold at each corner. Bake again for 20 minutes. Display on the plate stand.

Above and below: *The completed mirror and detail of the crazy quilting.*

4 Place the white block in the freezer for a few minutes, then grate it finely, directly onto the blue pearl square.

5 Roll a 2mm (¹⁄₁₆in) layer of raw sienna and cut it into 2mm (¹⁄₁₆in) strips. Place the strips on the burnt sienna square to form stripes.

6 Roll 3mm (⅛in) layers of pearl and black. Cut two 2mm (¹⁄₁₆in) strips of each and stack them, alternating the colours. Trim the ends. Cut thin slices of the resulting cane and place them densely, but in random directions, onto the raw sienna square.

7 Roll a 3mm (⅛in) snake of ultramarine blue. Then roll a 3mm (⅛in) layer of gold and wrap it around the snake. Use a craft knife to trim the ends, cut thin slices and place them on the beige square at more-or-less regular intervals.

8 Photocopy the mirror frame template (see opposite) at 154 per cent to the final size of 19cm (7½in) square. Cut out the numbered patches with the craft knife and divide them evenly between the "fabrics". Make sure that the numbers on any one fabric are not too close together.

9 Referring to the template and working directly onto the mirror, piece the patches together. The outer edge of the frame should be about 6mm (¼in) from the edge of the mirror. Bake for 20 minutes. When the clay and mirror are cool, remove the frame from the mirror. Clean the mirror thoroughly and glue the frame onto it.

6

special occasions

valentine heart plaque

This amazing, blazing heart will leave no doubt as to your intentions, so give it away with care! Bits of torn clay are applied as in a collage and make the heart look as if it's glowing from within.

Materials & equipment:
- Standard equipment and supplies (see pages 9 and 15)
- Royal Blue, Mother-of-pearl (2 blocks), Fluorescent Yellow, Golden Yellow, Orange, Fluorescent Red, Red, Black (2 blocks) and Bordeaux polymer clay blocks
- Contrasting ribbon

1 Make and lay the template over a 1.5mm (¹⁄₁₆in) layer of royal blue and cut out the heart shape using the heavy outline as a guide. Trace the template lines onto the clay (see page 15).

2 From one-sixteenth block of mother-of-pearl, roll a sheet as thinly as you can. Tear the sheet into pieces no larger than 12mm (½in) on any side. As you tear each piece, place it along the inside heart outline (refer to the main photograph as you build up the heart) so that the major part of the torn piece faces inwards to the inside. Continue applying pieces, overlapping them a little, until the inside heart is outlined in mother-of-pearl. Place one or two torn pieces of mother-of-pearl on each of the short lines around the inside heart. These are the bases of the spikes.

3 Prepare and tear the fluorescent yellow as Step 2 and place the pieces slightly overlapping the mother-of-pearl ones facing inwards from the inside heart outline. Then place torn pieces to overlap the mother-of-pearl spike bases, moving outwards.

4 Repeat Step 3 with golden yellow, orange, fluorescent red, red and bordeaux in that order. (The pieces placed on the spikes should be progressively smaller.)

5 Next, trim the royal blue clay to form spikes around the torn clay spikes. (The pieces do not need to be uniform.) Then lay the spiky heart onto a 1.5mm (¹⁄₁₆in) layer of mother-of-pearl. Trim the mother-of-pearl sheet into a smooth (but not symmetrical) heart shape, leaving 3–7mm (⅛–¼in) around the spike tips. Cut 9mm (⅜in) strips from a 1.5mm (¹⁄₁₆in) layer of royal blue. Use the strips to outline the mother-of-pearl heart, trimming and smoothing any awkward joins as necessary.

Photocopy this template at 133 per cent

6 Cut 2.5cm (1in) strips from a 3mm (⅛in) thick layer of mother-of-pearl. Then, from the strips, cut 2.5cm (1in) high triangles with narrow bases. Gently place the triangle points between the heart spikes (you may want to move or adjust them, see photographs), leaving the bases to extend over the edge of the royal blue border a little. When you are satisfied with the arrangement, press them into place.

7 Next, place the heart on a 1.5mm (¹⁄₁₆in) thick layer of black clay. Trim the black layer and the white triangle bases evenly with the royal blue border. Then cut 6mm (¼in) strips from a 3mm (⅛in) thick layer of black clay. With one cut edge pointing upwards, arrange the black strips around the outside edge of the heart. Press the black strips into position and smooth any joins neatly with your fingers.

8 ▽ Make a hole about 3mm (⅛in) in diameter in the top of each of the two heart lobes. Roll 4.5mm (³⁄₁₆in) diameter balls of black and press one ball onto the tip of each of the heart's spikes. Bake the heart assembly for 20 minutes, leave to cool, then thread a contrasting ribbon through each of the holes and tie it at the top of the heart.

decorated eggs

My daughter and I baked many batches of cookies with the insides of these eggs. I hope you too can turn egg decorating into a family activity to enjoy all year round. Leftover canes from other projects can be used for these eggs.

Materials & equipment:

- Standard equipment and supplies (see pages 9 and 15)
- Clean, dry egg shells (refer to general instructions)
- Polymer clay blocks (see individual eggs)
- Drill fitted with a buffing wheel (optional)
- Gloss glaze (optional)

General instructions

1 To prepare the eggs before decorating, blow them first, rinse the shells throughly and leave to dry completely.

2 Roll a 1.5mm (1⁄16in) layer of scrap or new clay 2.5cm (1in) wide or less. Beginning at one end of the egg, coil the clay strip around the egg, gently smoothing the joins and trim away the excess at the other end. Gently press the ends to find the original holes in the shell. Repierce at both ends with a wool needle. (If the shell has only one hole, water may become trapped in the egg and a shell with no holes at all will have little bubbles in the clay that form over the original holes.) Bake for 20 minutes.

3 For a shiny finish, sand the baked egg with increasingly finer grade sandpaper and polish with a buffing wheel fitted to a drill, if desired. Do not sand or buff eggs with surface treatments.

4 Decorate as desired, repierce the holes and bake again for 20 minutes. You can glaze finished eggs, but make sure you sand them carefully first or every surface dent and fingerprint will be accentuated.

Note: If you choose to quench your eggs (see page 16), you will find that the hot egg sucks up the cold water very loudly. Just blow out the water. Refer back to the preparation and baking instructions above for individual eggs unless otherwise stated.

ROSEWOOD EGG

Make a cane as for the Dark Necklace (see Steps 1–6, page 50). Wrap the resulting square canes with a 3mm (1⁄8in) layer of gray clay followed by a 3mm (1⁄8in) layer of rosewood. Reduce the cane to 2cm (3⁄4in) square. Apply three rounds of slices to the widest part of the prepared egg in a diamond fashion. Reduce the cane to 12mm (1⁄2in) square. Apply slices of this cane to the longer end of the egg. Use triangular trimmings from the original oval cane to join at the centre of the top and bottom.

Rosewood Egg

Clockwise from top left: *Forget-me-not Egg,
Ladybird Egg, Gold Outline Egg,
Rosewood Egg, Pink Stony Egg,
Victorian Rose Egg, Tesserae Egg and
centre: Blue Modern Egg.*

VICTORIAN ROSE EGG

Prepare a rose cane as for the Victorian
Fireplace (see pages 34–5). Reduce to
12mm (½in) square. Place three rounds
of slices diamond-fashion around the
widest part of the prepared egg. Reduce
the cane to between 9mm (⅜in) and
6mm (¼in) square. Continuing the

diamond pattern, use these slices to
cover the remainder of the egg.

FORGET-ME-NOT EGG

Make a forget-me-not flower cane about
18cm (7in) long as for the Mother's Day
Cards (see pages 104–5). Make the

leaves in both colourways, then make a
3mm (⅛in) diameter orange snake about
18cm (7in) long. Bake the flowers, leaves
and snake for 5 minutes. While these
pieces are still warm, cut into 3mm (⅛in)
slices. Cover a prepared egg with a 3mm
(⅛in) layer of white or translucent clay. ▶

Yellow & Turquoise Egg

Crazy Quilt Egg

Pink Stony Egg

Rosebud Egg

GOLD OUTLINE EGG

Prepare a cane as for the fuchsia-centred Tiled Night-light Holder (see pages 62–3). Reduce the cane to 12mm (½in) square. Apply slices in a diamond fashion to a prepared egg, leaving about 5mm (³⁄₁₆in) between slices at the widest part, reducing the cane as you approach the ends. Bake for 10 minutes, then fill the spaces between tiles with gold clay, leaving the gold clay a little proud of the surface. Bake again for 20 minutes and sand to smooth.

PINK STONY EGG

Make the cane as for the Stony Hair Slide (see pages 44–5). Cut into 3mm (⅛in) thick slices and cover the prepared egg, matching the stripes wherever it is possible to do so.

CRAZY QUILT EGG

Prepare polymer clay fabrics as for the Crazy Quilt Mirror (see pages 94–5). Cut irregular fabric pieces and arrange on a prepared egg. Do not sand or buff.

Purple & Silver Egg

ROSEBUD EGG

Cover an unprepared egg shell with white clay. Bake for 20 minutes and sand. Make the rose cane as for the Rosy Bathroom Jar (see pages 84–5). Apply 3mm (⅛in) slices to the egg and bake again for another 10 minutes. Check that the rosebuds are secure. If not, glue them back on again with extra-strong adhesive glue.

PURPLE & SILVER EGG

Prepare a purple, yellow and silver cane as for Tiled Night-light Holders (see pages 62–3). Reduce the cane to about 9mm (⅜in) square. Cover a prepared egg with cane slices, laid in rows.

Gold Outline Egg

Ladybird Egg

Blue Modern Egg

Tesserae Egg

YELLOW & TURQUOISE EGG
Tint translucent clay pieces with various shades of yellow, ochre and light turquoise. Next, prepare a mokume gane assembly (see page 20), separating the layers with gold leaf. Cover a prepared egg with the trimmings of this assembly.

BLUE MODERN EGG
Prepare a cane as for Tiled Cutlery (see pages 80–1) and reduce to between 12mm (½in) and 15mm (⅝in). Cover a prepared egg with cane slices.

LADYBIRD EGG
Cover a prepared egg with 1.5mm (⅟₁₆in) layer of green clay. Roll to smooth. Prepare a cane and black dots from a 6mm (¼in) and 3mm (⅛in) clay snake as for Ladybird Light Switch (see pages 92–3). Reduce the cane to 4cm (1½in) in diameter. Referring to the photograph above for placement, press four slices around the wider part of the egg to look as though the ladybirds are crawling in different directions.

Reduce the cane to 2cm (¾in). Nestle four slices between the larger slices, both above and below them. At the

longer end of the egg, place four more slices, trimming as necessary to meet at the end of the egg. At the shorter end of the egg, fill the space with one slice. Press large black dots into the large slices and small black dots into the smaller slices. Do not sand or buff this egg.

TESSERAE EGG
Prepare square tiles as for Tesserae Bangles (see pages 48–9). Cover a prepared egg with a 3mm (⅛in) thick layer of beige. Press the square tiles densely into the uncured beige clay.

mother's day cards

You can change or rearrange these bouquets to fit any size or shape of card that you can find. Alternatively, pierce the flower plaques and hang them from contrasting ribbons, then use them for ornaments or gift tags.

Materials & equipment:

- Standard equipment and supplies (see pages 9 and 15)
- Translucent, Orange, Blue, Yellow, Green and Light Green polymer clay blocks
- Cards with heart-shaped cut-outs (available from craft stores)

1 Make a 1.5mm (¹⁄₁₆in) diameter snake of translucent, bake for 5 minutes and slice into 3mm (⅛in) lengths to form dots. Roll a 1.5mm (¹⁄₁₆in) layer of translucent about 12mm (½in) in width. Bake for 5 minutes, then cut two 3 x 9mm (⅛ x ⅜in) pieces of the layer to form stripes. These are the vase decorations.

2 From 3mm (⅛in) layers of orange and blue, cut rectangles measuring 25 x 9mm (1 x ⅜in). Press the dots made in Step 1 into the orange rectangle. Press the two stripes from Step One across the width of the blue rectangle near to one end of it. Trim to square up the edges. Bake for 5 minutes.

3 To make forget-me-nots, roll a 3mm (⅛in) snake of yellow about 2.5cm (1in) long. Wrap with a 3mm (⅛in) layer of orange. Reduce the resulting cane to 1.5mm (¹⁄₁₆in) in diameter to make the flower centre.

4 Blend equal parts of blue and translucent together. Make six to eight 1.5mm (¹⁄₁₆in) diameter snakes of the blend to the same length as the flower centre (see Step 3). These are the flower petals. Lay the petals so that they touch each other along the length of the flower centre until it is completely surrounded by petals.

5 For roses, cut a 2.5 x 4.5cm (1 x 1¾in) piece from 1.5mm (¹⁄₁₆in) layers of orange and yellow. Stack the yellow layer on the orange and taper both edges. Beginning at one of the narrow ends, roll the layers together so that the orange covers the entire outer surface. Reduce the resulting cane to measure 7–8mm (¼–⅓in) in diameter.

6 To make the leaves, roll a 6mm (¼in) diameter snake of green, about 2.5cm (1in) long. Cut the snake in half lengthwise, insert a thin strip of light green, reassemble the halves, trim any excess light green and reduce the new assembly to 3mm (⅛in) in diameter. Pinch the cane on two sides to give it a lens shape. Repeat these instructions using light green as the original snake and inserting a thin layer of green.

7 Bake the flowers and leaves for five minutes. While they are still warm, cut 3mm (⅛in) slices of all the canes.

8 Trace the heart-shaped cut-out from the card onto a clean sheet of paper. Cut out the shape to use as a template. Lay a 3mm (⅛in) layer of translucent on the baking surface. Use the template to cut two hearts from this.

9 ▷ Working on the baking surface and referring to the photograph for placement, press the vases from Step 2 onto each heart. Arrange and press forget-me-nots and dark leaves into the clay around the orange vase. Then arrange and press orange roses and light leaves around the blue vase. Lay the template over the hearts again and trim, if necessary. Bake the hearts for 20 minutes and leave to cool. Glue the hearts onto the cards so that they peek through the heart cut-outs.

halloween party favours

These eerie, glow-in-the-dark, bloodshot eyeballs are gruesome and a little scary, which makes them perfect for children's Halloween parties. Children love these eyeballs – some adults do too, although they may not admit it.

Materials & equipment:
- Standard equipment and supplies (see pages 9 and 15)
- Glow-in-the-dark polymer clay block, scraps and bits of clay for the irises and little black pieces for pupils
- Toothpick
- Ribbon or leather necklace string
- Gloss glaze and paintbrush (if not supplied with glaze)
- Block of floral foam or the strong lid of a cardboard box
- Artist's paintbrush, size 0000
- Red acrylic paint

1 First, clean your hands thoroughly then break off one quarter block of glow-in-the-dark clay for each eyeball. Pinch off a little to reserve for the iris. Roll the clay into a ball.

2 Swirl together one or two colours for each iris plus a pinch of glow-in-the-dark. Break off a chunk about the size of two peas and roll it into a ball. Place on top of the ball from Step 1 and squash very gently. Use your fingertips to push the clay out into a round, dome-shaped iris. Roll a 3mm (⅛in) ball of black and press it onto the centre of the iris, flattening it gently.

3 Hold the eye so that you are looking at its side. Use the toothpick to pierce it through its middle from front to back, but about 7mm (¼in) above its equator. Make a hole large enough to thread ribbon or a leather string through it. Bake for 20 minutes.

Left and opposite: *Close-up of the eerie eyes and the luminous eyeballs and other traditional halloween party decorations.*

4 Put the toothpick into the hole and hold the toothpick as you paint the eyeball with gloss glaze. Push the end of the toothpick, with the eyeball still on it, into the block of floral foam or a strong cardboard box lid and then leave the eyeball to dry.

5 Paint tiny, awful-looking, squiggles using red acrylic paint to resemble blood vessels around the iris of the eye (see photographs). Join the vessels into larger, similar ones that run further out from the iris and continue merging the blood vessels until they join at the back of the eye. Leave to dry as before. (If you make a mistake, you can gently scrape the acrylic paint away from the glazed surface and start again.)

6 Cover the eyeball with gloss glaze again and leave to dry. String the eyeball onto a piece of ribbon or leather and tie to make a necklace. Finally, dangle the eyeball near a bright light for 15 seconds or so, then take it into a dark place and enjoy its spooky luminosity.

Note to grown-ups who plan parties for children:

- Making scary eyeballs can be a good halloween party activity, but only under adult supervision. Divide the clay and cut the ribbon or leather beforehand so that the children will not have to handle blades or scissors. Make sure that all the children wash their hands first before handling glow-in-the-dark clay because it picks up dirt easily and won't glow as well as it could.

- Use inexpensive paintbrushes but make sure the bristles come together at a point with no strays and use a water-based gloss glaze. It takes longer to dry, but it doesn't smell as strong as solvent-based glazes. Use small paper plates as palettes to hold the red acrylic paint.

- Let the children enjoy other party activities while you (the adult) bake the eyeballs and leave them to cool thoroughly away from small hands before they are strung!

holiday ornaments

Let the sun shine through these star ornaments and they will look as beautiful as stained glass. The two snowflake designs are just to get you started, so don't limit yourself to these ideas. You can vary the arrangement of the clay cut-outs to make every one different.

Materials & equipment:

- Standard equipment and supplies (see pages 9 and 15)
- White and Red Golden polymer clay blocks (for snowflakes); Transparent Blue, Transparent Orange, Transparent Yellow and Anthracite (for stars)
- Pattern cutter tool sets which include circles, hearts, flowers and drop shapes (sizes 4mm/³⁄₁₆in, 7mm/⁵⁄₁₆in and 10mm/³⁄₈in)
- Eyepins, for hanging
- Gloss glaze (for stars)

SNOWFLAKES

1 To make the snowflake ornaments, from a 3mm (⅛in) layer of white, cut seven x 10mm (³⁄₈in) circles, 18 x 4mm (³⁄₁₆in) circles, 24 x 7mm (⁵⁄₁₆in) drops and 18 x 4mm (³⁄₁₆in) drops.

2 Roll a 3mm (⅛in) layer of red golden at least 10cm (4in) square. Place this onto the baking surface. Centre the template provided over this layer and trace the lines (see page 15). Clean your hands before you touch the white clay again.

3 Using the project photograph as a guide, place a 10mm (³⁄₈in) circle in the centre of the red golden layer. Surround the centre with 10mm (³⁄₈in) circles centred on the six radiating lines. Along each line, place two 4mm (³⁄₁₆in) circles

and one 7mm (⁵⁄₁₆in) drop with the point facing outwards. Place a 7mm (⁵⁄₁₆in) drop on each side of the first drop. On top of each drop and at its base, place a 4mm (³⁄₁₆in) drop pointing in the same direction.

4 On top of the 10mm (³⁄₈in) circles around the centre and straddling each pair, place a 7mm (⁵⁄₁₆in) drop pointing outwards with its base about halfway between the inside and outside edges of the circles. These drops will line up between the traced lines. On top of each drop and at its base, place a 4mm (³⁄₁₆in) circle. Press the stacked motifs gently to make sure they stick together. Cut away the red golden background layer using the 10mm (³⁄₈in) circle cutter.

5 For the second snowflake, from a 3mm (⅛in) layer of white, cut seven 10mm (³⁄₈in) circles, 18 x 4mm (³⁄₁₆in) circles, six x 12mm (½in) hearts, six 10mm (³⁄₈in) hearts and six x 10mm (³⁄₈in) flowers.

6 Repeat Step 2.

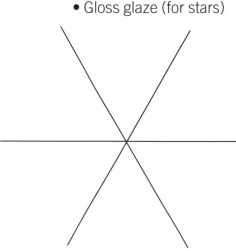

Guide for snowflake – photocopy at 133 per cent

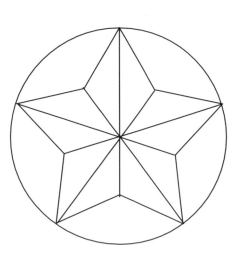

Star template– photocopy at 133 per cent

7 Using the project photograph as a guide, place a 10mm (⅜in) circle in the centre of the red golden layer. Surround the centre with 10mm (⅜in) circles centred on the six traced lines. Along each line moving out from the centre, place two 4mm (³⁄₁₆in) circles and one 12mm (½in) heart with its point facing towards the previous 4mm (³⁄₁₆in) circle. On top of each heart and at its base, place a 10mm (⅜in) heart.

8 On top of, and centred between a 10mm (⅜in) circle and the next 4mm (³⁄₁₆in) circle, place a flower. Then, on top of and at the centre of each flower, place a 4mm (³⁄₁₆in) circle. Repeat for the other five branches of the snowflake. Cut a

circle of red golden clay around the snowflake using a circle or biscuit cutter or with a craft blade. Bake the snowflakes for 20 minutes.

9 Finally, glue an eyepin to the back of the snowflakes to hang them, if desired.

STARS

1 Following the project photograph, from 3mm (⅛in) layers of transparent blue cut the background to the stars. From 3mm (⅛in) layers of transparent orange and transparent yellow, cut out the templates for the star points. Arrange on the baking surface. Press an eyepin into the middle of one of the points with the eye peeking out from the clay.

2 From a 1.5mm (¹⁄₁₆in) layer of anthracite, cut strips 2mm (¹⁄₁₆in) wide. With these strips, cover every join between the pieces cut from the template. Trim as necessary. Bake for 10 minutes at 10–20 degrees lower than your normal baking temperature. Turn the piece over and cover the joins on the other side with anthracite strips as above. Then wrap the outer edges of the piece with a 6mm (¼in) strip of anthracite clay. Smooth the joins and bake for 20 minutes as above. When cool, paint the sections with gloss glaze on both sides and leave to dry.

Above left and right: *Snowflake and Star Holiday Ornaments.*

useful information

The products used in this book are available at craft stores, do-it-yourself stores and department stores. If you cannot find a product, please contact the distributor for a retail location near you that carries the product you need. For polymer clay sources worldwide, look for this page on the internet: http://www.heaser.demon.co.uk/poly clay/polyinfo/htm.

In the United Kingdom:

Atlascraft Limited
(Cernit)
4 Plumptree Street
The Lace Market
Nottingham NG1 1JL
Telephone: 0115 941 5280,
Fax: 0115 941 5281.

Edding (UK) Limited
(Sculpey, Granitex and Premo)
Merlin Centre
Acrewood Way
St Albans, Herts AL4 0JY
Telephone: 01727 846 688.

Harrison Drape
(drapery hardware)
Bradford Street
Birmingham B12 0PE
Telephone: 0121 766 6111.

Inscribe Limited (rub-on gilding compound)
The Woolmer Industrial Estate
Bordon
Hampshire GU35 9QE
Telephone: 01420 475 747,
Fax: 01420 489 867.

Staedtler (UK) Limited
(FIMO and FIMO products, and metal leaf)
Pontyclun
Mid Glamorgan
Wales CF72 8YJ
Telephone: 01443 237 440,
Fax: 01443 237 440.

In the United States of America:

American Art Clay Company
(push-moulds manufacturer, FIMO products, rub-on gilding compound, tools and books)
4717 West 16th Street
Indianapolis, IN 46222
Telephone: 317-244-6871.

Clay Factory of Escondido
(polymer clay and videos featuring millefiori techniques with Marie Segal)
750 N Citracado Parkway #20-23
Escondido, CA 92029
Telephone: 619-741-3242;
Fax: 619-741-5436
e-mail: clayfacto@aol.com.

JASI
(manufacturer of the JASI Cane Slicer)
PO Box 40219
Pasadena, CA 91114
Telephone: 626-794-1530
http://members.aol.com/polyannie.

Kemper Mfg, Inc
(manufacturer of pattern cutters, blades, clay guns and sculpting tools)
Box 696
13595 12th Street
Chino, CA 91710
Telephone: 909-627-6191
(Kemper Tools are available in the UK, USA and 29 other countries. Please write for a list of distributors in your area.)

Kunin Felt Co, Inc (felt)
380 Lafayette Road
Hampton, NH 03842
Telephone: 603-929-6100
(Kunin Felt is distributed in the UK and other countries).

Polyform Products (manufacturer of Sculpey, Granitex and Premo)
1901 Estes Avenue
Elk Grove Village, IL 60007
847-427-0020.

Prairie Craft Company
(manufacturer of Marxit® and for blades)
865 N. Hermitage
Chicago, IL 60622
Telephone: 312-421-6105
Online: http://www.prairiecraft.com.

Walnut Hollow
(wooden trinket boxes)
1409 State Road 23
Dodgeville, WI 53533
Telephone: 608-935-2341
(Walnut Hollow products are available in the UK at larger craft stores).

Wee Folk Creations
(polymer clay, books, tools and videos)
18476 Natchez Avenue
Prior Lake, MN 55372
Telephone: 612-447-3828.

Other supplies and equipment used in this book were from Mirrorcles, Cole Brothers, Atkinsons, HobbyCraft, Whitehead's and W.H.Smith, all in Sheffield, England. Glues used in the book were Super-glue by Loctite and Araldite (an epoxy glue).

Organizations:

The British Polymer Clay Guild
Meadow Rise
Low Road
Wortham, Diss
Norfolk IP22 1SQ
http://www.heaser.demon.co.uk/poly clay/guild/britpol.htm.

Canadian Polymer Clay Friends
(Les Amies canadiennes de la pâte polymère)
http://users.envise.com/clayamies.

New Zealand Polymer Clay Guild
15 Pascoe Avenue
St Albans
Christchurch 8001
New Zealand
http://homepages.ihug.co.nz/~zigza g/nzpcg.html.

The National Polymer Clay Guild
(USA)
1350 Beverly Road
Suite #115-345
McLean, VA 22101
USA
http://www.npcg.org.

Further reading & viewing

Books

Heaser, Sue. *Making Doll's House Miniatures with Polymer Clay*, London, Ward Lock and New York, NY, Sterling Publishing Co. Inc, 1997. Miniature accessories for every room of the house. There is a good source list for miniature enthusiasts and much technical information that can be used for polymer clay work in general.
Making Polymer Clay Jewellery, London, Cassell, 1997.
Making Miniature Dolls with Polymer Clay, London, Ward Lock and New York, NY, USA, Sterling Publishing Co. Inc., 1999

Jeffcoate, Chris & Jackie Kuflik. *The New Sugarcraft Course*, London, Merehurst Limited, 1997 Ruffles, bows and other constructions designed for cakes can be recreated in polymer clay and used to decorate boxes, frames and name plaques.

Kato, Donna. *The Art of Polymer Clay*, New York, NY, USA, Watson-Guptill Publications, 1997 This book is well illustrated with step-by-step photographs and many, many beautiful examples of the techniques described in it.

Maguire, Mary. *Polymer Claywork*, London, Lorenz Books, 1996.

Roche, Nan. *The New Clay*, Rockville, Maryland, USA, Flower Valley Press, 1991 The subtitle of this book is *Techniques and Approaches to Jewelry Making* but it includes much more than jewellery-making and has clear descriptions and diagrams of techniques that can also be applied to all kinds of polymer clay work.

Westrope, Adrian & Pat Trunkfield. *Sugar Embroidery*, London, Merehurst Limited, 1996 The "Patchwork Bag" cake in this book was the inspiration for my "Rosy Bathroom" Jar design. Many of the techniques used in this book are transferrable to polymer clay.

index

Videos
In a series of videos produced by GamePlan/ArtRanch, 2233 McKinley Avenue, Berkeley, CA 94703, telephone: 510-549-0993, Tory Hughes shows her techniques for imitating semiprecious stones, and more.

Look for Sue Heaser's videos: *Master Artisans – Polymer Clay Series: A Medley of Jewelry Techniques; Master Miniaturists – Kitchen Miniatures with Polymer Clay; Master Miniaturists – Dining Room Miniatures with Polymer Clay*. These are available from Mindstorm Productions, 2625 Alcatraz, Suite 241, Berkeley, CA 94705, USA, telephone: 800 400 7099 and fax: 510 644 3910 (http://www.mindstorm-inc.com.).

Magazines
Magazines are a good source for designs and new techniques. Look in your local newsagent's shop for polymer clay designs and instructions in doll's house, jewellery and bead, as well as general craft magazines.

Two jewellery magazines that are published in the USA regularly carry polymer clay articles:

Jewelry Crafts, 4880 Market Street, Ventura CA 93003, USA. (http://www.jewelrycrafts.com.).

Bead and Button, P.O. Box 1612, Waukesha, WI 53187, telephone: 800 533 6644 or 414 796 8776; fax: 414 796 1615. (http://www.kalmbach.com/bead-button.html.).

Acknowledgements

Many thanks to the following suppliers for the products used in this book:

Atlascraft Limited for the Cernit used in the Ribboned Christmas Tree, Sunset Silhouette Picture, Ruffles Name Plaque and Mother's Day Cards.

Eberhard Faber for the FIMO used in the Art Deco-inspired Teaset, Victorian Fireplace, Grandfather Clock, Curious Cat, Stony Hair Slide & Earrings, Dark Necklace, Nautical Flag Box, South Seas Cruet Set & Napkin Rings, Ladybird Light Switch, Sun & Sea Wall Clock, Easy Picture Frames & Candle-holder, Tiled Cutlery, Valentine Heart Plaque, Holiday Ornaments (Stars) and Halloween Party Favours.

Edding (UK) Limited for the Sculpey III used in the Sea Treasures Brooches, Tesserae Bangles, Fantasy Fish Fridge Magnets, Football Name Plaque, Clown Cat Trinket Box and Holiday Ornaments (Snowflakes).

Harrison Drape for the limed oak drapery rod and finials.

Kemper Manufacturing Inc. for pattern cutters, blades, ball stylus, and texturing and sculpting tools.

Kunin Felt for felt used in the Nautical Flag Box and Clown Cat Trinket Box.

Marie Segal and Edding (UK) Limited for the Premo Sculpey used to make the Shiny Earrings, Tiled Night-light Holders, Crazy Quilt Mirror, Drapery Finials and Rosy Bathroom Jar.

Polyform Inc. for samples of Sculpey Super-Flex.

Staedtler UK for metal leaf used in the mokume gane designs and finials.

Walnut Hollow for the wooden trinket boxes.

With special thanks to:

Sue Heaser, thank you so much for your encouragement, for copious information on miniatures and polymer clay mosaics, and for showing me the wonders of the curved-blade craft knife.

For inspiration, teaching and setting a very high standard for me to live up to, thank you to polymer clay artists Maureen Carlson (she introduced me to polymer clay), Alex Curtis, Allison Gallant, Donna Kato, Mary Maguire, Margaret Reid, Nan Roche, Hen Scott and Marie Segal; and to Karey Miller Navo and her writers and designers at *Jewelry Crafts* magazine.

Charles, thank you for always saying "Of course you can", for all the help you gave on the graphics and for the many father–daughter trips you took to the Botanical Gardens so that I could work.

Thank you Mom and Dad for a lifetime of encouragement, good examples and belief in my abilities, and for many hours of playing with your grand-daughter so that I could work.

And thank you, my grown-up, three-year-old daughter Eva for the polymer clay slugs, snails, worms and sparkly things you made for my book, and for your patience with your preoccupied Mama.

Finally, to Nina, Jane, Lisa, Mark, Dave, Lee and Mike, thank you for taking my work and words and turning them into this beautiful book.